Weaving
Dreams

Weaving Dreams

**NOEL DONEGAN
& LUZ JAVA**

POOLBEG

Published 2008
by Poolbeg Press Ltd
123 Grange Hill, Baldoyle
Dublin 13, Ireland
E-mail: poolbeg@poolbeg.com
www.poolbeg.com

1 3 5 7 9 10 8 6 4 2

A catalogue record for this book is available from the British Library.

ISBN 978-1-84223-334-4

Typeset by Patricia Hope in Sabon 11.5/15.5

Printed and bound in the UK by
CPI Mackays, Chatham ME5 8TD

Dedicated to the memory of our fathers
Noel Donegan
Alton Java

And the memory of our niece
Rachel Dunne

They provided the threads to
weave our dream

Contents

1

The Good Samaritan

Noel's Story

I sat at the office desk, my body slumped and head bowed. Tears trickled down my cheeks and fell onto the blank sheet of paper in front of me. I was not sobbing or making any sound but the unstoppable tears burst through as the course of my sorry existence ebbed and flowed through my tired and tormented mind.

How had it come to this? The question begged for an answer, but searching for the answer only increased the terrible pain that was pulsating violently inside my head. "Stop, please stop!" I pleaded, crushing my skull between my hands. So much hurt, pain and guilt, suppressed and buried deep within myself, just could not be contained any longer and was now bursting to the surface like an erupting volcano, engulfing and suffocating me. Each resurrected memory and every unwelcome thought was accompanied by excruciating pain, a pain that was battling to suppress the truth.

I needed air. Somehow I managed to get to my feet. Holding my hands on my head for fear that letting go would surely cause it to burst open, I made my way out of the home office and through the front door of my house. I wandered aimlessly into the countryside.

I don't remember how I got there or how long it took, but somehow I walked from my home in Two-Mile Borris in Tipperary and arrived at Thurles train station, a walk of about four miles. It was December 2001 and Christmas was fast approaching. I had fled the house without my coat and now, with the cold rain pouring down relentlessly, my shirt was soaked through and it stuck uncomfortably to my skin. Without thinking or caring, I started to unbutton it. Perhaps subconsciously I hoped that all of my problems and all of the pain could be discarded as easily as that shirt.

I wanted to feel *new*. I wanted to start again, to wake up and find that the mess that was my life was only a bad dream. But life is not like that. Every morning I awoke to the nightmares and every night I fought against the reality as I tried to sleep. It was a messed-up, mixed-up existence and it had left me physically and mentally exhausted.

The heavy unrelenting rain had resulted in the platform being less busy than was usual, with passengers having sought shelter inside the station's waiting-room. It was a desolate scene that created a terrifyingly surreal moment. Standing alone on the platform, I found myself blending into the canvas, as the pouring rain and dark grey sky combined to paint a flawless monochrome landscape, capturing perfectly the colour and tone of my ever-darkening mood. I was outside of myself looking in and what I saw pushed me over the edge of sanity.

I was *alone*. I was a nothing, a nobody, a liar, a fraud. The floodgates had opened and I berated myself with every insult imaginable as the disgust at who I had become consumed me. My demons had escaped and, freed from their shackles, they showed no mercy as they made themselves known to me. Every face they revealed was my face and every silent scream they made came from my mouth. There was no escape, for how can you escape from yourself?

This mental flagellation was abruptly interrupted by the station's loudspeakers as they crackled noisily into life with the announcement that the Dublin train would be arriving shortly. The sound of the train, carried on the wind, could already be heard in the distance. Looking down onto the tracks, a thought from nowhere entered my mind. I suddenly realised that the cure for my pain was ringing in my ears and staring me in the face. I wondered why it had not occurred to me before. It was so simple.

I smiled for the first time that day as a wave of euphoria washed over me. I had found my escape. This tired body, tormented mind and broken heart would at last find peace in the everlasting sleep that only oblivion can bring. It was *perfect*.

Smiling, I walked along the platform in the direction of the approaching train. It must have been no more than a few hundred yards away when I crossed the yellow line that marks the safety boundary and positioned myself close to the edge of the platform. There was no time to think; all that mattered was this moment and my command over it. My final act in this world would be one of my own choosing.

Little by little, I worked myself ever closer to the tracks, only stopping when I felt the edge of the platform beneath the balls of my unsteady feet. It was a perilous position – a strong gust of wind might easily have blown me from my slippery perch and onto the tracks and yet, to my confused mind, it was so exhilarating. In this moment, seconds from my impending death, I had never felt so alive. For the first time in more than ten years I was in control of my life – *my life*. The words resounded inside my head as I looked towards the train, which was almost upon me. Looking skywards and with outstretched arms, I threw my head back in resignation and I inhaled a final breath deep into my lungs. As I exhaled this final taste of life I raised my heels from the platform's edge and, leaning forward, I let myself fall towards the tracks and into the path of the oncoming train.

At that very moment a sharp tug on the collar of my half-opened shirt delayed my fall just long enough for an arm to go swiftly around my chest and pull me back. It must have happened in a split second but to me it seemed to take place in slow motion. Turning my head, I looked directly into the eyes of the man who was holding me. "Don't do it, son!" he said through gritted teeth.

Instantly I reacted by grasping his hand, which now had a firm grip on my belt.

"Let me go or I'll bring you with me!" I shouted back at him in a mindless rage, and I meant it. Struggling against his hold, which he was not prepared to surrender, I finally managed to break free but by now the train had pulled into the station and was coming to a stop. My chance had gone.

"Listen to me, son," he continued, "there are solutions to every problem." I did not answer or pay him any attention but somehow the suddenness of his intervention had brought me back to a state of something resembling reality. He placed his hand on my back and said, "C'mon, son, let me buy you a drink or a coffee. You must be freezing in that wet shirt."

I don't know why, but for some reason I walked with him, this stranger, this Good Samaritan, as he ushered me towards the exit of the station.

As we sat over the coffee I took notice of him for the first time. He was in his late fifties and casually dressed in jeans and a duffle coat. His face was hard and weather-beaten like his hands, in stark contrast to his manner and voice, which were cultured and refined. He spoke with an accent that was hard to place – it was Irish but with a sort of French twist to it. He made several attempts at small-talk before finally asking the question, "Why would you want to do a foolish thing like that?"

"Why not?" was my sarcastic reply. What did he know about me or my life? My head was throbbing and as I raised my hands to massage my temples I looked at him and said, "Sorry." This mess was not his fault.

"How did you get yourself into such a state, son?" he asked, his tone not the least bit intrusive. On the contrary, it was genuine and concerned. He had saved my life and, although I was not feeling particularly thankful to him for that act, he nonetheless deserved an answer.

But where could I begin? How could I answer his question – the very same question I had asked myself only a few short hours ago, a question which had almost resulted in my demise? He might just as well have asked me to tell him the story of my life for the past twenty years, for that's how long it had taken for me to be worn down into this sorry state, to be worn down into nothing!

"There has to be a reason," he said, filling my mug with coffee and breaking the silence that had met his question.

So I began.

2

Living the Lie

I began where I had begun earlier that day by recalling my marriage back in 1982, a lifetime ago. I married young to a woman who was almost eight years older than me. We had met when I was seventeen years old and married when I was twenty-one.

Maybe it was because of the age difference or maybe it wasn't, but it soon became clear to me that we were two very different people with very different ideas of what mattered in life. For my part, the acquiring of possessions or the power of status would never define who I was. I wanted the meaning of my life to be measured in *happiness*, not by the size of my bank account. And what greater expression of that happiness is there than the love found in the caring, loving relationship of a husband and wife and all of the good things that relationship will bring about? For that love is theirs and theirs alone and no matter what else happens in their life, no one can take that away from them.

But I was wrong. Love has to be received and not just given; it must be expressed and it has to be felt; but above all, it has to be real. All that I felt coming from my wife was coldness and a distance in the physical side of the relationship, which seemed to worsen by the same degree of understanding I gave to it – which was a *lot*. I had always considered sex and love to be inseparable – the ultimate sharing of intimacy sacred to the couple and an unrestrained giving of oneself. But to love fully and with a passion and for that love to feel as though it is being *facilitated* and not enjoyed or returned was very disturbing to me.

Perhaps it was my fault. I started to doubt myself and the doubts plagued me. I had been a virgin when I married and now I wondered, *Am I an inept lover, incapable of making her happy?* I was twenty-two years old and so confused. I bought books, read magazines and did anything to try to make it right, but none of it had effect. Any attempts to talk about it were always met with the same answer: "I'm just different from you; I don't need what you need." So I learned to back off. I tried to understand her words; perhaps she was right and I was expecting too much.

"But how could longing to feel wanted be too much to ask for in a marriage?" Now, in thanks for my under-standing and adapting to her ways, it seemed that unless I instigated the lovemaking, it just would not happen. I didn't blame her or harbour any ill feelings towards her because of this – this was who she was and I knew she was not being like this just to spite me. But I would be lying if I did not admit that knowing this did little to ease my feelings that our relationship was somehow *incomplete*.

The ideal I held so close was dead and truly buried. On those occasions when we did have sex, it felt to me as if that was all it was – just *sex*. I never felt love sharing our bed. I tried to reason that it did not matter; time would change things and, if not time, then I would. It is truly amazing how delusional you can become when you so want something to be as you dreamed it would be.

Although my passion remained fixed on the relationship and trying to salvage it, it seemed to me that her real passion was ignited when buying new clothes and talking about style. The attention such things drew to her appeared to feed a desire to set herself above others and gain their approval by hearing them say how well she looked. Style, it appeared to me, seemed to define her. It was a behaviour that I discovered she had learned from a very early age. I would hear at family gatherings that she did not just go to school, she went to *Mount Sackville private school*; or that her brothers had not just got promotions, they had got *big promotions*; or not that we have a car but, *Oh, we have three cars*. It was always about boasting and trying to show yourself off as better than everyone else. These facts, it seemed, were mentioned not to inform anyone, but rather to impress them.

I reasoned that she had been conditioned – a victim of this behaviour – and I had hoped that once out of that environment, she would adopt different values. However, even at this early stage I must have known that the marriage was a failure, but I did not want to acknowledge or admit it. So many people had advised me against the marriage but, with youthful arrogance and pride, I had refused to listen to them. I would not let them see me fail. I would make this marriage work, whatever the cost.

I buried the hurt and the desire deep within me – for if I did not have to think about it then I would not have to face it. I strongly held the belief that whatever went on within the marriage should remain within the marriage and so, tied to my convictions and out of loyalty to the relationship, I began to live the lie. To all on the outside it appeared as though I was the happiest man in the world with the perfect wife and the perfect marriage. In reality, I felt like a possession – nothing more than a clothing of flesh and blood – and like all her other clothes and possessions I felt as though I was just something to show off. I was *her perfect husband* and something to make other people envious. I played along with this charade for if nothing else we were *united* in the lie and foolishly I hoped that one day it could be truth. Crazy as it now sounds and considering all that was wrong in the marriage, she was still my wife and I was not going to betray her in any way.

Our son was born in April 1986 and our daughter followed in March 1989. Their births were my salvation. My marriage was more bearable because I could channel all of my love into them, and they would and did return it to me. They were the joy of my life and gave me the happiness I so desperately sought. Their being in my life compensated for and allowed me to ignore the emptiness I had felt before their arrival.

Money was not a major problem at this time. It's not that we were flush, but my job as a hairstylist meant that

I could earn enough money to keep things ticking over. In the late 1980s and early 1990s, like most people, we were doing well by managing to keep our heads above the water. However, one morning while contemplating a move to Australia in search of a better life for the kids, an envelope fell through the letterbox with the rest of the post. It contained a letter that would change my life and our relationship forever, but not in the way I had envisioned. It was from the prize bonds office and I smiled and thought to myself, *That's lucky, we've won £100. It will be nice to treat the kids.* But when I looked closer I could hardly believe my eyes. It was not one hundred pounds we had won – it was *one hundred thousand pounds!* This was 1992, and £100,000 was a life-changing sum of money.

They say it never rains but it pours and for us it was now pouring down by the bucket-load. I had just licensed a hairdressing invention that I had created to L'Oréal for worldwide distribution and it was providing us with some very welcome extra cash. This combined with the prize bond win meant we had more money than we ever dreamed we would have.

It took several days for the reality of this windfall to sink in but, after the initial excitement had died down, it was time to discuss what we were going to do with the money. I suggested to my wife that, as we were both hairdressers, we should buy premises and fit them out as a hair and beauty salon. We would not need a loan so the overheads would be very manageable and in time the business would provide for all our needs, including the bigger house we would require as the children got older.

My suggestion, however, fell on deaf ears. In no uncertain manner I was reminded that the prize bond was in *her name* and that what *she wanted* was to buy a bigger house and a car. It was folly and I said so, but there was nothing that I could do to stop her.

I had well and truly been put in my place. I wondered in that moment how she might have felt had I retaliated by arguing that, if we adopted her definition of *hers* and *mine*, then the house we were living in was mine. I had been the one working to pay the mortgage on my own for seven of the previous ten years. I had also bought the furniture, paid the bills and provided for anything else that we needed.

I am not going to lie and say that the prospect of moving to a much-needed bigger house was not exciting and something to look forward to – of course it was, but the lost opportunity to do so much more with the money and the manner in which I was put down left a very bitter taste in my mouth and it hammered another nail firmly into the coffin of an already fatally wounded marriage.

We sold the bungalow – our home for ten years – and bought a bigger four-bedroom house in Palmerstown, only a short walk from our old house. It was a disastrous move. The house was in excellent condition, having only recently been built. The previous owner, who had very tastefully decorated it, had spent very little time living there before putting it up for sale. It had triggered alarm bells in my head as I wondered, *Why would someone spend all that money and then put the house up for sale?* But my wife wanted the house and that was that.

We were only living in the house a few weeks and settling in when my worst fears were realised. A problem neighbour who was very seriously disturbed made living in the house a nightmare. At first the abuse was levelled at my wife and then at me but when the children became victims of the harassment it was time to call the police. It made little difference, however, as even after the intervention of the police, the non-stop annoyance and aggravation continued day and night. With tempers running high and the safety of the children paramount in my mind I realised that it could only end badly if we continued to live there. After spending a little over a year in that house we decided to put it up for sale.

Logic should have dictated that we look for a house with a price tag equivalent to the amount of money that we would receive from the sale. We had been mortgage-free and there was absolutely no reason why we should not keep ourselves in that position. But logic and reason played little or no part in our life now. Money was being spent like there was no tomorrow and apart from the money that was tied up in the house from the profits of the sale of our bungalow, the invention and some of the prize bonds win, the rest was *gone*. So many times and on so many different occasions I tried to curb the spending, knowing that if we did not then soon we would be left with nothing. Any conversations on the subject would usually develop into a row and rather than waste my breath or expose the children to them, I just stood back and waited for the inevitable to happen. Everything was happening too fast.

In the midst of all of this chaos, I received the news that my father, whom I loved dearly, was in a critical condition in Dublin's Mater Hospital. His second heart bypass had been a failure and, with the news that he was dying, I dropped everything and rushed to the hospital. When I got there he was already on life support and I knew I had to prepare myself for the worst. It was a time for family. My mother, my brothers, my sisters and I found comfort in each other as we held vigil by his bedside and awaited the inevitable.

I must have been in the hospital for no more than thirty minutes when my mobile phone rang. It was my wife. I thought she was calling to ask how my father was and perhaps how my mother and the rest of the family were holding up. But, no: she called at this most delicate of times ordering me to come home immediately because the neighbour was adding more blocks to our boundary wall. I could not believe my ears. My father was dying, my mother and the rest of my family were distraught, and she was arguing with me and telling me to get home and deal with the neighbour. I hung the phone up in disgust but not before the youngest of my three sisters, Christine, who had been standing beside me and heard the entire conversation, had taken it from me and told her just what she thought of her for calling me and unnecessarily burdening me at this time.

A few minutes later she rang again, only this time I was told that the children were frightened and very upset because they were now being harassed. She told me that if anything happened to them, it would be entirely my fault. It was blackmail and I knew it but I could not afford to take a chance with the children's welfare. It was a heart-wrenching decision to leave my father's side but I knew what he would have wanted me to do. When I arrived at the house I discovered that the children were fine. Yes, they were upset but it was nothing that she could not have dealt with by herself. Her call had been nothing more than a drama to get me home to protect her *wall*.

Mercifully my father did not die that afternoon. He died the following day and I got my chance to hold his hand and say my goodbyes. But this precious time had almost been denied me, all because my wife thought a wall, and not my dying father, deserved my attention.

It was a numbing but defining moment for me. What she had done – to drag me away like that from my dying father's bedside – was heartless and I could not and would not forgive her for it. I did not know her any more, but more than this, I now knew that I did not love her any more. Whatever sparks of hope I clung to for our relationship were well and truly extinguished that day. I might easily have ended the marriage there and then and had it been just her and me, I would have. But it was not just about her and me, there were the children to consider. They would be devastated had I left and I did not want that. I did not want them suffering the fallout of a broken home.

And so I swallowed my pride, hid my disgust and buried another part of who I was in order to function in this lie that my life was becoming. What choice did I have?

When we had lived in the bungalow and before the prize bond win, I had been in control of the financial side of our life. What we had was what we could afford and although it was a modest standard of living, it was at least that – *living*. There had been a time for work and a time to relax. But since the prize bond win, a new unsustainable lifestyle had been entered into and every waking moment had been spent trying to keep it going. The house was now up for sale and the search to find a new one had begun.

Unable to switch my mind off from recent events and consumed by the worry of how we could afford this forced move, I was not sleeping. The lack of sleep was affecting my concentration and I began to feel particularly unwell. For the first time in my life I felt an uncontrollable nervousness take hold of me and it shook my confidence and affected my work. Hairdressing is a job where you need to be at the top of your game; there is no room for error. But errors were creeping into my work and the more it happened the more nervous I became. Finally I could not face the thought of being that close to someone. I would often find myself cutting or drying a client's hair and the sweat would just start pouring from me. I could not continue like this and had no choice but to go on sick pay and eventually a disability payment from the social welfare. The marriage, the financial situation, everything in my life was falling apart and I did not know how to cope with it.

Having sold the house in Palmerstown, we bought a new and even *bigger* house in Lucan and with it came a whole load of new pressures, to be piled one by one upon my shoulders. Financially the house was well and truly out of our reach. It required a mortgage to purchase it and, with no savings to our name, securing a mortgage was nearly impossible. It was an especially worrying time for me because money had already been paid into the property in the form of the initial deposit and down-payments on a conservatory and the conversion of the garage into living space. The mortgage was required for completion. I sent application after application to the lending institutions and finally, at the eleventh hour and just when it seemed all hope was lost, I managed to secure the mortgage.

But as one financial crisis was temporarily solved, other more stressful ones would raise their ugly heads. With only one salary coming in and as it was doubtful that I would be able to resume the work to bring in that income, I was really worried about how we were going to meet the mortgage repayments. Luckily – depending on how you viewed it – I had passed a kidney stone while in work and had been carted off to hospital in an ambulance. I had been able to use this event to disguise my real reasons for needing sick leave and to buy myself some time to try and get mentally fit again. If I could not continue working in hairdressing, I would need another source of income and so I was participating in a "start your own business" course run by FÁS. I enrolled on the course with a view to starting a consultancy for inventors, but this business idea was in its infancy. It was in the feasibility study stage and nothing was guaranteed.

There was also another worry as to where the many thousands of pounds required to finish the interior and make the house habitable were going to come from. My wife's solution? "Borrow it – you have friends with money.

Borrow it and we will pay it back when your new business idea takes off." As if it was the simplest thing in the world to do. I would have preferred to move into that house without a single fitting in the interior rather than borrow money from friends, but what else could I do? We were already committed financially and if we had backed out at that stage, we could have lost thousands of pounds. Then there were the kids to consider. They had endured a horrible experience by being terrorised in their last home and now they faced the prospect of moving into a house that was nothing but an empty shell. Apart from it being unhealthy, I just could not do that to them.

I kept asking myself why we had put ourselves in this stressful position when we could easily have bought a smaller house for cash and concentrated on the quality of our life – not the quantity in it. Other than the children, there was no joy in my life any more. Every day was just another stress-filled episode in a life that was running out of control.

With no other avenues available to me and with the pressure being piled on from every quarter, I borrowed the money. I became a liar. I lied to our friends and talked up the business in order to convince them to give us the money. It was so easy for her to say "borrow the money" and to spend it, but I was the one who had to do the asking. I am not for one moment trying to deny my culpability in borrowing that money. It was wrong and something that I would later live to regret, for many different reasons. Now, not only was I living a lie in my marriage; I had also become a lie to myself as, day by day, week by week, month by month and year by year, I learned to tell the lies a little better. I had got so good at telling the lies that eventually I even managed to convince myself that they were true.

It seemed that no matter how much money we borrowed, it was never enough. There was no such thing as waiting until we could afford to buy all that was needed to finish the house or even considering if we could afford them in the first place. Nothing could wait; everything had to be done now. By the time the house was completed, we had borrowed tens of thousands of pounds over and above the mortgage. It was frightening to be accumulating this debt but more frightening was the realisation that working at a job nine to five was not going to clear it. Something big needed to happen and it needed to happen fast.

With no money available to set up the business, all my hopes were resting on positive feedback from a game I had invented. I had entered into an agreement with a company in the UK who specialised in licensing new toys and games and gave them the rights to exploit it. The thought that this game could fail was something I would not allow myself to consider. As the weeks and months passed, the expected breakthrough was not happening and the game idea was starting to go cold. Mortgage arrears were mounting up and, with no income, we found ourselves falling deeper and deeper into debt.

Everything was spiralling out of control. By this stage I'd had enough of the lies and the stress was really starting to show on me. It came to a head one afternoon when I point-blank refused to borrow any more money. The monthly car repayments, along with all of the other bills, had fallen into arrears and the current month's instalment was now also well and truly overdue. "I don't care," I snapped. "Sell the car and while you're at it sell the house and buy one that we can afford!" It was time to come clean about our situation and find a solution to paying back this borrowed money, which was like an ever-tightening noose around my neck. If it meant selling the house, then so be it; at least then we could pay our debts and be free of the lies and I would be free to look for a regular job and earn an honest living.

I was already attending a specialist in Saint James's Hospital about stomach problems that I knew were brought on by the stress of the life we were living and had been prescribed tablets to stop excessive stomach acid. I started to believe that unless I actually dropped dead in front of her, I was never going to get respite. *Is this it, have I become nothing more than a device – a means of procuring money to feed a ravenous lie?* I asked myself; but I already knew the answer to that question.

"I really don't care what you do, but I am not borrowing any more money and that is that!" I went on, happy that at last I was putting a stop to this madness. She did not reply; she just grinned at me and walked away. I knew I had not heard the last from her on this subject.

The following afternoon I arrived home from the city centre and noticed that the car was not in the driveway. I presumed that she was out with the kids but when I entered the house she was coming down the stairs to meet me. The loan company had repossessed the car and she was fuming. To be honest, I wasn't bothered – we should never have bought the car and perhaps this was a lesson well learned.

My complacency, however, was short-lived when I realised that our son was upstairs and had heard every word of our heated exchange on this subject. I ran upstairs to his bedroom and she followed. He was visibly upset and I knew he'd been crying. "How could you do this to us, Dad? It was so embarrassing – all of the neighbours were looking at the car being taken away," he blurted. "This is your fault, Dad, for getting us into debt," he continued sobbing as his mother sat beside him on his bed. I looked at him and, seeing the anger in his eyes, I knew he had been told something bad about me. "Ma said that if you had a job like everyone else, then none of this would have happened," his words stuttered through the tears. I looked at him, unable to reply for fear that if I did, I might not have been able to contain the hatred I was feeling towards his mother in that moment for what she had just done.

There were any number of excuses she could have made to a thirteen-year-old boy about why the car had been taken away. She could have said that it needed repairs or that we wanted to have it checked out before we drove it again, but I could see no reason why she had to upset him by exposing him to a lopsided view of *our problems*. Seeing him like this did not just hurt me – it also demonstrated how easily the children could be turned against me. What other reason could there be for what was happening? I could have argued with her in front of him, let him hear my side of the story, but I could never do that to him. I was not going to use him to justify and referee an argument between his parents. I had played out this lie, this sham of a life and marriage, for everyone else and now was not the time for his young fragile mind to be assaulted with a truth it was not capable of understanding.

Whether I liked it or not, I had played a part in the creation of this illusion called a happy family, which for all its faults and lies had one certain truth at its core – the children were happy. If only my son had known how much I yearned to have a *normal job*, to have nothing else to worry about except clocking in and clocking out and a wage packet at the end of the week. But how was he to know that the amount of our debt was now over one hundred thousand pounds and that a *normal job* was never going to pay that off?

She had won; she could see how upset I was to see him like this and it demonstrated very powerfully that if she lost her house and her status, then I could lose the only thing that really mattered to me – my children. I was not going to lose my children. With my spirit finally broken, the car was back in the driveway the following day and more money was added to our ever-increasing debt.

Disaster seemed to be my companion when it came to buying houses. The previous house had been a nightmare to live in and now we discovered that our new house was structurally defective. Not only had the kitchen floor split in two, but we noticed noxious smells in the house emanating from the utility room. We discovered that there was no soil vent pipe provided for the waste coming from the downstairs toilet and, as a result, toxic fumes were now venting freely into the house. It was a very serious problem. The structural defect, though annoying and disappointing, was not as worrying as the health risk posed, especially to the children, by the inhalation of the sickening vapours.

After months of trying to avoid the problem, the builder finally agreed to repair the house; however, his definition of a repair and mine were two very different things. Even if the house had been repaired, a new certificate of compliance would have to be issued and it in turn would have a devaluing effect on the property. We could not live in the house as it was and I could not in all good conscience paper over the cracks and sell it on to some unsuspecting family. It was the builder's fault and I wanted him to purchase it back from me for its market value. A lengthy legal battle ensued, finally coming to a conclusion in the High Court. We were sitting in the corridors of the court waiting for the case to be called when the builder finally saw the light and agreed to purchase the house back from us. It was a victory but a hollow one for me. Now I had to start searching for yet another house for us to live in – *our fourth house* – and I knew that could mean only one thing: borrowing more money.

The court case had added to the huge amount of stress that I was already living with on a daily basis and I started to feel really unwell. I could not sleep any more and eating caused me terrible stomach and chest pains. My mind and my body were telling me to stop but crisis after crisis made that impossible. First my grandmother died; then my son suffered a ruptured appendix that nearly killed him; and as if this was not enough, my mother had a near-fatal brain haemorrhage. I was physically exhausted and mentally drained, not to mention being sick to the pit of my stomach from the stress, but I had to keep going. If I stopped now, the whole house of cards would come crashing down and my children would be the real victims. So I did what I had learned to do so well – I sucked it all in and buried it, convincing myself it would all work out in the end.

We decided to buy a house in Tipperary. It was a 3,500-square-foot house in a beautiful setting. For me the appeal of the house lay not in its size but in the fact that I was physically and mentally putting some distance between myself and all of the problems. This was of course delusional thinking, but it gave me some space to breathe. Though larger in size, the price of the house was comparable to that of a four-bedroomed house in Dublin. It would not add anything more to the problem now facing me of once again trying to secure a mortgage – or so I thought. Because of the arrears accumulated from the last mortgage and the bad payments record for the car, our credit rating was appalling. The house was being built on a staged payments basis and with the last stage nearing completion, the final payment would soon be due. The proceeds from the sale of our previous house had already been exhausted and still I could not get a mortgage anywhere to complete the purchase. To make matters even worse, once the lenders found out that I was on a back-to-work allowance scheme, it was a non-runner.

The stress at this time was becoming almost unbearable. We were living in rented accommodation while waiting for the house to be completed and we were borrowing the money to pay for the rent. Without being able to make the final payment on the house, there was now a very real danger that we would lose all of the money that had already been paid. All of this worry was placed squarely on my shoulders and I must have made appointments with and spoken to about a dozen lenders while my wife spent her time making plans as to how she was going to decorate and fit out the house.

In a final desperate bid to secure the mortgage, we called into a broker in Thurles, whose offices we passed on our way back from doing some grocery shopping. We told them our problem and, unbelievably, they said that they might be able to help. I don't know how they managed it, and to be honest we didn't really care, but somehow it looked as though they would get the mortgage through. It was such a relief to secure the mortgage that thinking about how we were going to pay for it was something that could wait for another day. If somehow I could get my business started, then perhaps it would all work out in the end. The important thing was that we had the house and in time we could furnish it and make it into a home.

But who was I fooling; nothing in my life was ever that simple. With the mortgage having just been secured, the pressure was piled on to find even more money. Most people in our position would have been content to have secured a mortgage and resigned themselves to furnishing the house as best they could and over the years with whatever money they had available to them. But we were not living our lives like most people. That house *had* to be fully furnished from top to bottom before we set foot in it. I often wondered how she could just switch off and appear to be oblivious to our financial situation. An already huge overdraft from the bank had provided the funds for the essential fittings, but the *essentials* would never be enough. The usual rows ensued, the usual threats were made and, as usual, I went looking for the money. I had gone past the point of caring.

With the borrowed money, the house could now be fully fitted out and life, it appeared to me, went on as usual for her. I had started to experience the beginnings of panic attacks, waking suddenly in the night, my heart racing and the sweat pouring out of my body. Soon after this, I suffered a painful case of shingles. My body and my mind were slowly submitting to the years of stress that had been placed upon them. But I was shown no pity or mercy. The demands were relentless and even my hardened stomach could not believe what she asked for next.

With the children in the back of the car, we pulled up outside the house. We were there to inspect the property and to see how the fitting out was progressing. As I brought the car to a stop, she asked, "Have you booked the holidays?" She knew as well as I did the Trojan effort it had taken and the huge amount of stress encountered in order to purchase this house. Now she was asking me, as if we had not a care in the world, if I had booked our holiday. I was livid but with the children in the back of the car, I kept my rage in check.

"Sorry guys, but there will be no holiday this year. We need to spend our time sorting this house out," I told the kids, sparing them the truth that we did not have any money.

The words were no sooner out of my mouth than she added, "Do you hear that, kids? No holiday this year." Anyone who listened to the conversation that ensued would have formed the impression that I had money or that I could easily get it, but was not prepared to spend it for their fun.

The kids were once again being exposed to our arguing and even though I was trying to disguise the arguing as best as I possibly could in the circumstances, it appeared to me that they were being used as leverage. But by this stage and after all of the previous stress and strain, I was simply too worn out to argue or fight back. If they wanted their holiday, they would get their holiday, and to hell with the consequences. I really didn't care any more. I borrowed the money for whatever was wanted and told her to enjoy it while she could, because soon payback day would come and then all that we had would count for nothing.

I hated my life. I was a stranger to love, held ransom to money, devoid of hope and without a moment's peace. Everyone was looking for me now. The bank was looking for the overdraft to be cleared and the building society was threatening legal proceedings because of the arrears that had built up. Everyone that we had borrowed money from over the years now wanted their money back. Yet in the face of this we still had to spend more.

Christmas came and brought with it more outrageous demands. "I want two sets of clothes for the kids for Christmas . . . I want more Christmas decorations . . . I want to buy more presents . . . I want to buy my clothes and I want three Christmas trees, one for the conservatory, one for hall and one for the gallery." Want, want, want! There appeared to be no end to it. The rows were getting worse and with our voices raised, the kids could hear everything. I did not want them exposed to this. I was reaching breaking point and there was nowhere to run and nowhere to hide. I turned the mobile off, did not answer the phone and refused to open the bills.

3

Break Down

The shirt by now had dried into my back and, as I brought my story to an end, I asked the man who had saved my life, "Does that satisfy your curiosity?" In twenty years of marriage, he was the first person I had ever opened up to about my problems. He had not interrupted me, not even once in the telling of my tale, and now it looked like he was searching carefully for the words to his reply.

The smallest of smiles broke out on his face as he said, "This is not about satisfying my curiosity, son. It's about you satisfying a need to get this off your chest and getting the help you so obviously need."

"Help? And who can help me now, who can give me back twenty years of my life and undo the hurt and the lies, who can erase the guilt and take the pain away? Who?" I asked, challenging him for an answer.

"I don't have the answers, son, but there are people out there who do – professional people who deal with this kind of thing every day. You don't have to deal with this on your own."

He was a good man and meant well, but I didn't want to hear any more. I thanked him for the coffee and his time, and, after refusing his offer of a lift or to call someone to collect me, I said my goodbyes and started back home. I have often wondered who he was and on those occasions that I remember him I regret that I did not show more gratitude for what he had done.

"Where have you been? Look at the state of you." These words greeted me when I entered the house. Sitting with my wife in the front room I explained what had happened and how I had almost ended my life. I begged her to listen as I tried to explain how it had come to this and I hoped that maybe she would see that all of this nonsense had to end. She listened and made no comment. Then, standing up, she looked at me and said, "So why didn't you jump under the train and do us all a favour?" And with that she walked out.

So now I knew. As far as I was concerned, my life meant nothing to her. In that moment I felt about as useless as it is possible to feel while still being alive. All the negative thoughts, the pain and the feeling of suffocation I had experienced earlier that morning returned. I decided that if she wanted me dead then I would willingly give her what she wanted. No one would pull me back this time.

With her words ringing in my ears and consumed by despair, I went into my office. I started tidying some papers that were strewn about the desk. I must have hit the computer mouse because the monitor suddenly lit up and I heard a strange sound that I had never heard before.

I was a relative novice when it came to computers. The one in my office was borrowed from a friend and I was using it to practise my skills and for email. He had also given me an installation disk for setting up web access and it contained a built-in messenger. Being of a curious nature, I had set up the messenger to see what it did but never actually got around to using it. It never seemed to work and I assumed that I had done something wrong with its installation. But now it sprang into life and the strange sound that I'd heard was the sound of a message someone had sent saying "Merry Christmas". Surprise was soon overcome by sarcasm as I typed the reply, "And what's so bloody merry about it?" A few moments later came the strange sound again, accompanied by the message, "Don't be like that. It's Christmas – you should be happy."

I can't recall what I replied to that message, but two hours later I was still sitting at my desk and chatting to this virtual stranger. In that two-hour period this person had somehow managed to calm me down and pull me back from the brink of self-destruction. They had given me their time and shown me the compassion and understanding that my wife just a few hours earlier would not. For the second time that day a total stranger had intervened to save my life and it was something even my troubled mind could not ignore. Maybe I was not as alone as I thought I was – someone was watching over me.

Before we finished chatting I discovered that it was a woman I had been talking to. Her name was Megan. At the end of our conversation, she told me not to think of doing stupid things again and that I must always remember how my children loved and cared for me. Finally, she said that I had better be at my desk the following day – she wanted to check in with me to see how I was doing. It might sound a very sad thing to say, but I had received more understanding and warmth in that two-hour conversation than I had received from my wife in almost twenty years of marriage. Maybe it was because we were anonymous – I could not see her and she did not know me – that I opened up so freely to her. It allowed me to overcome my inhibitions and not feel as though I was being disloyal by discussing my marriage and its problems with her.

When I had finished the chat I confronted my wife. "I know you don't give a damn about me – telling me to jump under the train has made that perfectly clear – but, sorry to disappoint you, that is never going to happen." I didn't give her a chance to reply or interrupt me. "I have had enough of you and this destructive relationship and I want to end this marriage now before it ends me." I was wound up and I needed to get this out of my system now. "I have been on the computer speaking to a total stranger for the past two hours. Have you any idea how sad it is for me to feel that I have received more understanding from her than from my own wife?" As I spoke those words, I really felt that sadness. "You can find some other fool to do your bidding from now on. All I ask of you is that you work with me to find the best way of explaining this to the kids and do what is best for them."

I did not want the children to know the real reason for our break-up, as it would serve no purpose other than to make a difficult situation even more unbearable for them. I did not know how we would explain it to them, but what I did know was that there would be absolutely nothing to gain from either of us entering into a *blame game*, forcing them to choose sides. They would be hurt no matter what we told them, but at all costs we had to let them know they still had both their parents who loved them dearly. I appreciated that it would take time for us to work through this and I was not going to suddenly up and go. I would stay there until I knew the kids were comfortable and understood and could make sense of what was happening. As soon as this was done, I promised her that I would pack my bags and get out of her life forever.

A nonchalant shrug of her shoulders made me feel as if she had dismissed me and what I had said as if it was nothing more than a demented flight of fancy. I was certainly demented – I was sure of that – but the only flight on my mind was one that would take me as far away from her as possible.

Over the coming weeks and months I spoke with Megan through the computer on an almost daily basis. It was food for my soul to know that someone cared enough to want to spend this time to talk with me. Here at last was someone who wanted to listen and who could give of themselves without wanting anything from me in return. The chats were a wonderful distraction that helped me to find a space where for an hour or two I could leave all my problems behind.

Weeks, then months, passed and still my wife refused to discuss with me how we were going to explain our splitting-up to the children. If she thought that this delaying tactic was going to change my mind, then she was wrong. It had taken so many years for me to come to this decision but remembering what she had said about me throwing myself under a train made it an easy one in the end. I could no longer bear to be in the same space as her and told her that if she would not face up to our problems, then I would do it for her. She would reply by saying that she needed more time and asked me not to leave until she could sort it out in her head. I agreed. I had put up with all of this nonsense in our life for almost twenty years, so a few more weeks or months were not going to make any difference. I never hid from her the fact that I was talking to Megan or that we had become good friends through our chats, which by this stage also included phone conversations, but I did agree on her request not to discuss it with anyone out of respect to her.

As the months went by, it became inevitable that Megan and I would have to meet. We were both curious to put a face to the voice and so we arranged to meet in Dublin. I did not hide this from my wife and felt no guilt for doing it. I had told her months before that we were finished and I was only living in that house and with her because she had asked me to stay until she had sorted herself out. Megan flew into Dublin from the UK and we finally met. It was a wonderful meeting and we learned even more about each other. She told me that she had worked on the police switchboard in the UK and had first-hand experience of dealing with people in distress. On the day when she had sent her first message to me, she had sensed from my reply that something was wrong. That was why she had kept me chatting; she knew I was a danger to myself and wanted to calm me down. I learned that she was unhappily married to an abusive husband and that was why she could identify so easily with me.

Our friendship was cemented that day and I would be lying if I said that we did not discuss taking it to another level. It would have been so easy to let ourselves go and submit willingly to our needs and desires. But the fact remained that I was married and so was Megan. Although every impulse in my body was telling me to do the opposite we did not enter into a sexual relationship that day. I was proud of that fact. I was proud that I had not totally lost who I was or my beliefs.

When I arrived back in Tipperary I told my wife what had happened – and, more importantly, what had not happened. She listened but I gauged by her reaction that she thought it was all just some fantasy I was making up in my head. Over the years I had taken and soaked up everything that had been thrown at me and I knew that she genuinely did not believe that I was going to go through with this split. Once again I asked her to please sit down with me and discuss our splitting up. My patience was running out and I needed to get on with my life. More weeks went by and still she was not taking me seriously. If I had to, I would explain to the kids on my own and as best as I could the reasons why I was leaving their mother, but I wanted to avoid that if at all possible. They deserved to have both parents tell them and reassure them that they would still have all of their mother's and father's love, no matter what happened.

At this time I made an arrangement to fly to the UK to see Megan. She wanted to see me and in fairness she had been the one to make the previous trip. Again I told my wife what I was doing and again she ignored what I was saying. We had agreed, for the sake of the kids, to tell them that I was going to see a football game. But while we were in the car on the way to the train station to see me off, she suddenly turned to the kids and said, "Your father's a liar – he is going to meet another woman." She had chosen her moment well. All of the time I thought she had been ignoring me and playing for time, she had actually been planning her move against me and now I felt that move involved turning my children against me. I was caught totally off guard and was shocked that she would subject the kids to this. *Does she not care that they are distraught and sobbing their hearts out at what she's just said to them?* I asked myself. It seemed her only concern was to try to show me up in their eyes. Sitting in a car at a train station was not the time or the place to tell them the real truth of what was happening.

I told the kids that what their mother had said was not the full story and that when I got back I would explain everything to them. I could have cancelled the flight and gone back home but that was what she wanted. All of my married life she had got her way and controlled me by using the kids, but not this time. It hurt me to leave for the plane and to see them crying as I left but I had to call her bluff. I had to let her see that it was over between us and that exposing the kids to our problems and upsetting them like that was not going to work any more.

It was good to see Megan again and over the course of the two days I was with her it became clear that we were falling in love with each other. We were two people in very similar circumstances, both looking for love and understanding. I hated leaving her and she was sad to see me go but I could not rest easy knowing how my children were being used. I had to sort it out.

When I got home I discovered that the kids had obviously been told a one-sided story in my absence. I could only guess that this had been done to make me look bad in their eyes. They had been told that I had accumulated a huge debt which had left us penniless and that I was now going to run away from the problem to a woman I was having an affair with, leaving them with nothing. The kids were so upset and started asking me, "How can you do this to us, Daddy?" A mutual friend of ours was also in the house and had been brought into the drama. Because I had agreed, at my wife's request, not to mention Megan to anyone, she was now using this against me. She claimed that she knew nothing about Megan until that day when I was flying to the UK. She had even set me up with this friend by allowing me to tell her – as my wife had requested – that I was only going to see a football match. This friend now thought I had been lying, and strictly speaking I was – but at my wife's request and for her benefit, not mine.

I tried my best to explain to the kids why we were splitting up but without going into the personal side of the relationship between their mother and me. It was a difficult task because without them knowing the personal side, they could never fully understand the reasons for the break-up. They were too young to know of such things and this was very much to my disadvantage. I also could not make it personal because I did not want to put them in the position of choosing sides. She, on the other hand, played her cards so very well. She had used Megan to make me look like a liar and a cheat and convinced the kids that, because I was the one who asked for the money we had borrowed, the debts were all my fault and that they would lose everything, including their home, if I left them. But as much as I tried explaining that I was not leaving them, I was leaving her, it just would not sink in with them. All they could see was that the family was splitting up and I understood them for thinking that way. I was damned if I stayed and I was damned if I left. I had to consider my position very carefully.

The children's welfare had to come before my wants and I did not want them thinking of me as this terrible man who it appeared their mother was making me out to be. I contacted Megan and told her what was happening. It was one of the hardest things I ever had to do but we both agreed that we would not pursue our friendship any further, for the sake of my kids and hers. They were the innocents in all of this. How could we ever have happiness knowing that any relationship we might have could hurt them so much?

Once again I had lost and the loss made me more depressed than ever. I had not just retreated to that torturous place inside my head I thought I had escaped forever – it was worse than that. Psychologically, from my perspective, she had gained the upper hand and my self-esteem dipped to new lows. I was trapped and there would be no escape unless I was prepared to risk losing my children. Megan, the angel who had supported me and lifted me out of the depths of despair, was gone.

Alone, with only my demons for company, the panic attacks returned with a vengeance. I wanted to run, to scream, to feel my body explode and scatter in a million pieces, never to be found again. I was paralysed with fear and dread of the things to come. My mind did the running that day – it fled reality and retreated to a place no one could reach, far from the deafening screams that only I could hear. My nervous breakdown was complete and Tipperary mental hospital received a new patient that day.

My mother and my eldest sister Lorraine travelled to Tipperary from Dublin on hearing the news of my breakdown. They later told me that my wife had found me in the office, with tears pouring from my eyes and staring blankly into space. She had called the ambulance and I was taken to Tipperary mental hospital. When they arrived to see me I did not know or recognise them. I was completely withdrawn and incoherent. I was seen by the consultant, given medication and brought to an isolation ward for observation.

Later that evening I was allowed to go home under the supervision of a psychiatrist, who prescribed drugs for me, including anti-depressants and sleeping tablets. The anti-depressants certainly helped and for a few weeks it seemed as though I had not a care in the world. The sleeping tablets knocked me out and for the first time in years I remembered what a full night's sleep felt like. As the weeks passed my powers of reasoning slowly returned. I resolved to get off the medication. It felt like I was being controlled and I did not like that feeling.

My fears of being controlled were confirmed when I overheard a phone conversation between my wife and one of her friends. She thought that I had been sleeping and had no idea I was listening outside the door. "Yes, you were correct. I was speaking to a solicitor and it was the right move to call the ambulance and have him signed in; it will count against him." Her voice was low and hushed. The rest of the conversation was a series of yeses and nos that made no sense to me but I had heard enough. It now appeared that my wife had not called the ambulance out of concern; it seemed she had called it on the advice of her friend and because it could put me in a compromising position.

I had just about got back on my feet, was finished with the drugs and attempting to tackle some of the problems that needed sorting when, once again, the topic of borrowing money was raised. I wanted nothing to do with borrowing any more money and point-blank refused to do so. Despite my illness, I was still determined to leave her and I told her so. She was mistaken if she thought I had taken leave of my senses and forgotten how she had given a one-sided account to the kids about the cause of what was happening. Despite all of our differences, I was not prepared to do anything behind her back and so I told her that Megan had been back in touch with me.

On hearing that I was not going to borrow the money and of my determination to leave her, she backed out of my study and into the hallway. Then, and with more than fifteen feet between us, she smiled at me – and then shouted at the top of her voice, "Son, quick, call the police! Your father is assaulting me!"

I just stood looking at her, totally speechless. This was a new low. My son came running down the stairs to see what was wrong. She continued her drama, repeating, "Call the police, he's mad – he just tried to put my head through the glass door."

The police were called to our house – one of sixteen houses in a quiet country development – completing the embarrassment to our family. I could not believe that this was happening. I have never broken the law and to this day I don't even have a parking ticket to my name. I stood there and watched, helpless, while she blurted out her lie so convincingly to the policeman and policewoman. A new fear gripped me: *What if they believed her?* The thought really scared me as I realised that, in this situation, it was just my word against hers.

When she had finished I finally got my say. I asked the police to consider what she had said and, taking into account my size and strength, did they really think she would still be standing there if I had intended doing what she had told them I was trying to do, which was to put her head through a glass panel in a dividing door? I told the truth about what had happened and suggested to the policewoman that it might be a good idea to bring her into one of the rooms and examine her body for any marks. I even volunteered to go with them to the police station and be charged if they found even one single mark or scratch anywhere on her body. With no marks to be found, it was obvious that the police had seen her call for what it was. They left.

That episode really frightened me. Maybe the next time she pulled a stunt like that, she would mark herself, and then what would I do? She had tried to paint me as a wife-beater in the eyes of my son and without a single thought as to how this would impact on him. Even when the police had gone, she continued to insist to him that I had assaulted her. It was an evil thing to do.

The rows continued, the police were called and again they could do nothing, as nothing had happened. The neighbours, however, were once again treated to a spectacle and I am sure that many of them thought, *there's no smoke without fire*. So even if she was not succeeding in getting me charged, these actions were certainly succeeding in destroying my reputation. God only knows what was being said to people about me when she met them in the street but I honestly could not blame them if they believed her, for she was so convincing.

Every time she called the police, more damage was done to my relationship with the kids. She would put on the tears and would try to make out that I was being abusive to her. The final straw came one Saturday morning in October 2002 when another row broke out about money. This time the arguing was so loud that there was no way that the children could not hear it. My son had run upstairs to his bedroom and my daughter was crying her eyes out in the conservatory. I guessed what my wife's next move was going to be, but this time I got there first. I called the police and asked them to come out immediately.

When they arrived, I told them, "I am sorry for involving you guys in our domestic situation once again, but as you can see there is a very heated argument going on here and the kids are very distraught by it." I was really embarrassed at having to call them, but I went on. "For the sake of the kids, I think it's best if one of us leaves the house for a while and, to be perfectly honest, I'm also very scared of what she will accuse me of next when she gets like this." That was the truth. I never again wanted to experience what she had put me through the last time when she accused me of assaulting her. "Please take note that I am not abandoning my home or my children. I am merely removing myself and in so doing protecting my kids from a potentially volatile situation." I wanted it fully understood that I was not abandoning my kids or my home.

"He's mad, don't listen to him! He's been locked up in a mental hospital and he chats to women on computers," she said, constantly trying to interrupt my conversation with the police. Her outburst, though unwelcome, seemed to demonstrate to the police the gravity of the situation and they applauded my decision, saying that no one could compel me to leave but, seeing how upset the children were, it would be best if one of us left until the situation calmed down.

My sister Lorraine and my brother-in-law Joe Dunne came to collect me and they brought me back to Dublin, where I stayed with my mother and Lorraine while I waited for the dust to settle. I had been gone from the house in Tipperary no more than a few days when I was served with a notice to attend Thurles District Court to defend an application made by my wife for a barring order against me – under the Domestic Violence Act!

I was horrified when I read it. How dare she make such an application! I had never laid a finger on her in my life. It was another attempt to destroy my name, to try to teach me a lesson not to leave her, and an opportunity to discredit me in the eyes of my children.

Lorraine loaned me the money to hire a solicitor and we both went to Tipperary for the court hearing. Thank God that the judge was wise and refused the order, as there were no grounds for granting it. He asked me to give an undertaking to keep away from the family home for a period of time in order to let things settle down. I readily agreed to his request, as this had been my intention when leaving the house in the first place. I breathed a sigh of relief. I knew it was unusual for barring orders not to be granted and I was glad that my wife had not been able to abuse me or the system as she had hoped she could. The judge gave me leave to visit the house on New Year's Day 2003 to see the children.

Although I was happy at this outcome, one thing kept nagging at the back of my mind and it was this. All that my kids could have assumed from my court appearance was that Mammy had to apply for a barring order against Daddy, because he must have done something wrong; but I knew in my heart that they would never hear from her that the barring order had been refused – thereby proving that Daddy did nothing wrong at all. Their flawed perception of me as a bad man and father would get further justification merely by the fact of my being in the court, even though my defence had succeeded.

In the weeks following the hearing, I tried on numerous occasions to talk to the kids over the phone but every time I rang, she told me that they were either out or that they did not want to speak to me. It was so frustrating.

I had never been this long away from my children and I missed them so much. Usually I would get them their breakfast or make them their lunch. Most days I was able to bring them to and collect them from school. I never missed a concert or a school meeting. I had always been there for them and played a very full part in their lives. This total lack of contact with them was driving me crazy.

I feared that in my absence further lies would poison them against me and I knew that everything that went wrong from here on in would have its blame laid firmly at my feet. After the refusing of the barring order, I could only conclude that she was bent on punishing me, even if that meant depriving her children of the love of a father who adored them.

Having given an undertaking to the court not to visit the family home until New Year's Day I had no option but to be patient and wait for my chance to see my kids again. It seemed to take an eternity but finally New Year's Day arrived and I found myself once again in the family home. It was so wonderful to see the kids and they were equally overjoyed to see me. It was meant to be my chance to spend some time with them but, within an hour of my arrival, she started her tricks again. With the kids listening, she said to me, "I want you to come back and stay." She could not even allow me this time on my own with the kids without using it for her own purposes. It was so selfish of her to mention this in front of the kids, who were obviously hoping that their parents would get back together.

"You know that is not going to happen," I replied and I told her it was inappropriate to be discussing it in front of the kids.

But she would not let it go. "I hope you're listening, kids, he does not want us any more. He would prefer to be with that bitch in Wales."

Once again she was upsetting the kids and involving them in something that should have been discussed privately between us. But she had to know what she was doing; she had to know how bad this was making me look in the eyes of our children. Her temper was rising. As she continued her verbal assault on me, memories of false accusations and police being phoned flashed through my mind. I suddenly felt very vulnerable. Her tantrum continued to escalate, to the point where she ordered me out of the house. Even though it was pitch black and I would be heading out onto an unlit country road, it was a better option than staying with her and leaving myself open to further false accusations. She had ruined my visit with the kids and I hated her for that.

I was gone about five minutes when my mobile phone rang. It was my daughter. She was crying, asking me to come back, because she was worried something would happen to me walking the pitch black country road. Her fears were well founded because, with little or no visibility, I had already fallen into a ditch. For this reason and because I could not bear to hear my daughter upset and crying like that, I returned and stayed the night.

Before returning to Dublin, and quite by accident, I discovered that my wife had changed all the locks on the house. She had got her father to change them and it sickened me to imagine what sort of message that had sent out to my kids. The full extent of how this could turn my kids against me was now plain to see and I needed to take action. With no other option, I found myself back in the District Court seeking access to the children. It was wounding to sit there and listen to her telling the judge that she was not preventing the kids from seeing me, that it was their own choice and that she was merely respecting their wishes. It did not take the judge long to establish that I was a good father but because of their age – my son was sixteen and my daughter was thirteen – he could not compel them to see me. It was not the result I was hoping for but I was not going to give up that easily.

I met Megan several times during this period and in the end it transpired that she could not go through with her plans to split from her husband. She was not the reason why my marriage had ended – that was going to happen with or without her – but it was sad that something that was good between us should end up coming to nothing.

Although I could not get to talk to or see my kids, it did not stop my wife phoning and annoying my family. She had phoned several members of my family, including my mother, asking them to convince me to go back to her. When I heard this I wondered what exactly was going through this woman's head. She had called me a liar and cheat, not just to my kids but to anyone who would listen to her. And yet here she was begging my family to convince me to go back to her. Not that they ever doubted me, but it was good that my family could now see her lies for what they were.

As the weeks went by, the separation from my kids became almost unbearable and most nights I cried myself to sleep thinking about them and remembering how I would never retire to bed without first tucking them in and kissing them goodnight. Although Lorraine and my mother were a great support to me and did everything they possibly could to help me get through this difficult time, I still found myself getting depressed and struggling to find reasons for continuing in this life if I could not be with my children. Life and death – I had already stood on the thin line dividing the two and looked headlong into the abyss. It held no fear for me, but if all that awaited us was the void, then what did all of this living count for? What was the purpose of a life of suffering if it all counted for nothing?

I got lost in the thought and soon found myself with pen and paper attempting to capture and hold onto a revelation that was being made known to me. When I finished, it felt as though I was seeing for the first time in my life. I had pushed back the darkness and with the light of life glowing within me I lay my head down and slept like a baby.

4

Butterfly Wings

I stood in the shower and let the water pour over me. It was cold water, icy cold, and it shocked me to the core. But I wanted to be shocked. I did not want my senses to be dulled or seduced by feelings of warmth or comfort. I was alive – more than that, I felt exhilarated – more alive than I had ever felt before. All of my senses were heightened, everything appeared so clear, every sound so crisp and every smell so potent. It was a wonderful sensation. I immersed myself totally in this moment, closing my eyes and surrendering fully to the feelings that were washing over me, flooding every part of my being with a new vitality and energy.

Was it possible? Could a silly little poem, a poem penned by me while in the depths of a suicidal depression, really change my life? The words of the poem went round and round in my head:

When butterfly wings are dry
They carry it to flight
Free it reigns in its domain
From chains that bound it tight

When babe inside its mother's womb
Is sacrificed to life
No remorse at this course
Yet now begins the fight

When butterfly wings are dry
Its beauty will unfold
A miracle of its own rebirth
From all that it has known

When all our living has been done
And breath we draw no more
Our true beauty will be revealed
Like butterflies we'll soar.

Now I understood. Life is a challenge; it neither offers nor accepts any guarantees. It is a titanic struggle on a magnificent voyage whose final destination is unknown. From the moment we leave – no, from the moment we are expelled from the comfort and safety of our mother's womb and forced to draw our first breath, filling our lungs with the food of life . . . it is from this moment that the struggle, the heroic fight, begins.

There are no constants. Like the butterfly, we evolve and change. Who we are and what we ultimately become is up to us. It is the innumerable choices and immeasurable decisions which shape our being and set the course for our Journey. The body we occupy is our vessel, nothing more than a different, more sophisticated Womb from that in which we travelled on our first Journey, on our very first voyage to an unknown destination, a destination we now call Life! No doubt we will make many more journeys on the road to enlightenment and who knows what wondrous adventures they may hold in store for us. But it is in the unknown that the real beauty of our existence is revealed, for we were not created *to know*. We do not have to live in or think in or be in any other moment or place other than that which we now occupy. We have the privilege of living in the *now*, living in the moment, forever propelled into the future, a future that our actions in the *now* will create. We step into a destiny of our own making, into a World not created by us but forever shaped by us. A World shaped by every single action of every single human being who has ever walked on this planet.

The power to shape my world was within me, but I would have to change. I would change like the butterfly and leave the ugliness of my past behind. I turned the water off and stepped out of the shower and there and then I made myself a promise. I promised that, just as the cold icy water had cleansed my body, removing the grime of the previous day, I also would cleanse my soul and my being from all the negative things that had taken hold of my life. I would let them wash away with the water and remove them from my life forever. I was going to start this day as I intended to live every other day of my life that would follow. This day was going to be the beginning of the rest of my life.

But never, not even in my wildest dreams, could I have imagined how truly amazing this day would be.

I could not tell you how often I have walked down O'Connell Street in the heart of Dublin City. Hundreds, perhaps thousands of times. But what I can tell you is that as I walked down O'Connell Street on the afternoon of 23 January 2003, it was a very different experience than those I'd had before. Usually I was just another one of the bustling crowd, a part of the human herd hurrying to their destination, finally getting from A to B, but with a head so preoccupied with the stresses of modern life that I would be unable to recall anything else about the walk other than knowing I had set out and arrived. You know that feeling when you seem to be on automatic pilot. You know you crossed the road but cannot recall actually crossing it. It's almost as if your mind has so much going on inside it that your brain has to prioritise what it allows you to control and what it needs to take charge of.

However, today I was not hurrying. Today I was in control. I was not part of the herd; I was apart and separate from it. I could observe it. The heightened sense of awareness that I had experienced earlier that morning had not deserted me. I stopped for a few moments at the end of O'Connell Bridge, at the junction with Bachelors Walk. I rested against the bridge and observed what was going on around me. As usual, people were busy hurrying to and fro. It was easy to imagine that some unseen force had ensnared and joined them with an invisible string, pulling them to where *it* wanted them to go. Everyone appeared to be caught up in their own little world, blinkered to anything that was not in their direct line of sight – looking but not seeing. How many of them were happy? How many of them were following a path not of their own making and experiencing a life contained by the motives of others? There is nothing wrong with being part of the herd if you are happy to be there, but I was not. I had been a part of the herd for too long and it felt good to be free and in control of my own destiny, whatever that destiny might be.

The lovely ornate clock that hangs above the main entrance to Eason's bookstore caught my eye. I had never really noticed it or appreciated it before and so I decided to go and take a closer look. Having satisfied my curiosity, I decided I could do worse things than go inside and browse the books to see if I could find something inspiring. I have always loved books and they have been good friends to me, offering advice, giving instruction, opening debate, setting challenges and opening doors to numerous worlds with endless possibilities. They have made me laugh, they have made me cry and they have on many occasions made me angry. All of them have enriched me in some way or another.

But the most extraordinary book that I ever encountered was the one I never read. For today, without ever turning one single page, it would magically and amazingly make me fall in love and change my life forever.

Eason's seemed particularly busy that afternoon and I almost decided not to go in. Busy means queues and I absolutely hate and have no patience for queues. Standing in line as if it's a privilege to give your money to someone else has never rested easy with me. However, with only forty euro in my pocket to last me for the week, it was highly unlikely that I would be tempted to buy anything and end up in the queues. As much as I love books, you can't eat one or wear one. It was a simple case of getting my priorities right. I decided that, as I was here now, I might as well go in and have a browse. Maybe I would see something I could buy next week.

Perhaps I had too many books in my collection because I was finding it unusually difficult to find one that interested me. Nothing jumped out at me from the shelf saying *read me*. I was looking in the self-help section, and usually an intriguing title or an interesting cover would grab my attention and arouse my curiosity, but not today. Then, and just as I was about to leave and try a different part of the store, I noticed a book. It was on the second row of the bookstand immediately to the right of the one that I was browsing. This book, along with several others, formed a group of about five. They had been wedged awkwardly in between others on the shelf, with their spines facing outwards. The particular book that had caught my eye did so for one simple reason: it was standing rather proud from the others in a rather precarious position. I could already visualise in my mind someone passing by and knocking against it, sending it crashing to the floor and in all probability ruining the hardback cover. I hate to see books messed up or destroyed, particularly new books. I reached out to take hold of it. My initial intention was to just push it back in, and then I thought, *Sure, I might as well take a look at it first.*

Precisely at the same moment that I began to reach for the book, I was distracted by what sounded like someone calling my name. Momentarily I turned my head in the direction from which I thought the sound was coming. In doing so, I turned away from the book on the shelf. Realising that no one had been calling me, I turned my head back. But it was too late. In those few seconds that my head had been turned, someone else, another hand, had reached for that very same book. Just as she was lifting it off the shelf, my hand collided with hers and the very thing happened that I had been trying to prevent – the book went crashing to the floor.

There then followed a series of embarrassing and comical events. Feeling a little embarrassed and in a reflex reaction, I said "Sorry." She also said "Sorry." Then, just as we had done seconds earlier, we both stooped and reached instinctively for that same book to pick it up from the floor – only this time we managed to bang our heads! Once again, with impeccable timing, we both said "Sorry," and once again we both found ourselves with our hands on that same book. This time I thought, *I'd best let her retrieve the book before I embarrass myself any further*. But would you believe it, she obviously had the very same thought and so we both relinquished our grip on the book and once again it went crashing to the floor. It was like a slapstick scene from a Laurel and Hardy movie. A further wave of embarrassment washed over me as I tried to recover my composure.

However, neither the embarrassment nor the composure lasted long, for both soon gave way to feelings of a very different nature. For as we both straightened ourselves from the stooping position we were in, our eyes met for the very first time.

I will never forget that moment. She was beautiful. Her alluring brown eyes, though soft and gentle, burned straight through me. There was no hiding, no defence against them, only total and wonderful surrender. For those few seconds, nothing else mattered, for there was nothing else, only this beautiful moment with this beautiful woman. She was Asian. Her hair was black like the colour of midnight and she wore it cut short in a tussled casual shaggy style, which accentuated her high cheekbones. Her lips were full and inviting; they curled up at the edges, giving her a permanent smile which was so cute and sexy. It was hard to gauge her age; her skin was the colour of gold and without lines. It was a happy face, a kind face and it was, oh, so beautiful. Knee-high boots were worn over a pair of jeans and matched with a denim jacket. The look may have been casual, but she was pure class.

"Let's come to a compromise," I offered, having finally managed to put my tongue back into my mouth and fixed my jaw back into position. "You can buy the book, so long as you let me buy you a cup of coffee." The words had leapt straight out without ever passing through my brain, though looking back now, this should not have surprised me. For it was not my head that was talking; the words were coming straight from my heart.

She smiled back at me; it was a face that was made to smile and though the smile was genuine, it could not disguise her shyness or the awkwardness she was obviously feeling at that moment. She was a contradiction. At that moment she seemed so timid, so vulnerable, and yet there was something incredibly strong about her. I waited for a reply to my offer of coffee but none came. She just kept looking at me, the smile still on her face. *Perhaps she does not understand English*, I thought to myself, *or perhaps she is just smiling at me and thinking, "Is this guy for real?"* Either way, I had a situation to rescue.

Maybe it was the newfound confidence and vitality I was experiencing, or maybe it was just down to the fact that I was not going to let this beautiful creature get away, but whatever it was, it spurred me to continue. "Okay," I said, "If it makes you feel any better, and just because I am such an understanding guy, you can buy the book and the coffee!" This time her smile widened and she laughed. *Phew, thank God for that*, I thought, more than a little relieved. "Seriously, I am just about to go for a cup of coffee and, seeing as we have already had a meeting of heads," I went on, rubbing the spot on my head where it had clashed with hers, "why not have a meeting of minds? Have a chat with me over that coffee; I would love the company." I held my breath.

"Okay, that would be nice," she replied in a soft exotic accent. For a moment, I just stood there looking at her. She had said "yes"!

"Great! By the way, my name is Noel." I offered her my hand.

"Luz," she replied, accepting it in hers.

"Nice to bump into you, Luz," I said, my hand once again going to my head.

"Me too," Luz replied, laughing.

"Look, it's getting pretty crowded in here, Luz. What do you say we go for that coffee now, I could really do with one?" My fingers crossed as I asked the question.

Luz answered "yes" and we made our way to the exit. As we walked through the store on our way to the exit I nervously put my hand in my pocket, trying to locate my forty euro. Relieved, my hand closed around it and I thought to myself, *Thank God I had not spent this*. But my relief was short-lived. Something else had dawned on me. It was now lunch-time. I just hoped Luz was not hungry and, if she was, I prayed she had a small appetite.

The Royal Hotel at the top of O'Connell Street is only a short walk from Eason's bookstore and seemed as good a place as any to have that coffee. It was only after I had suggested the hotel and as we were walking to it that the gravity of what I had just done hit me. Here I was, walking down the street with a woman – a complete stranger I had met only moments ago – and I had asked her to join me in a hotel for coffee! I am sure a lot of men have received a slap in the face for less. I often ask Luz, "Why did you not run a mile from me when I suggested that we go to a hotel?" Her answer never changes as with a smile she replies, "Angels come in all shapes and sizes, Noel."

We engaged in the usual small-talk as we waited for our coffee. When it arrived and as I poured for Luz, I asked her where she was from. "The Philippines," was the reply. I had never met anyone from the Philippines before and I told Luz that I would love to hear about her life there. I have often been told that I am a good listener and easy to talk to, but I never expected Luz to be as open with me as she was.

"Do you really want to know about my life Noel?" Luz replied, "It's a very long and complicated story."

I loved the way Luz spoke my name. Most people pronounce it as if it's spelt *Nole*, but Luz put the accent on the *el* and it sounded so nice.

"Complicated? Don't worry about complicated," I told her, "You're talking to Mr Complicated."

Luz smiled that beautiful smile of hers. She sat back in her chair and said, "Well okay, Noel, if you're really interested, then I'll begin."

5

Face of the Devil

Luz's Story

Lambajon, Baganga, Davao Oriental, Philippines

I was happy. I was a majorette and my twirler group had just won top prize in a national schools competition. It had been a gruelling parade. The scorching heat of the hot Philippines sun had been unrelenting as it burned into our skin and sapped our energy. But today, nothing could remove the smiles from our faces as we recovered our strength, resting beneath the welcome shade of the coconut trees that lined the perimeter of our school. The girls from my twirler group had occupied all of the available benches and so, with nowhere left for me to sit, I leaned against the post of a cottage just a little distance behind them. I was sixteen years old, as were most of the girls in my group, and our innocent laughter carried on the winds as we giggled with excitement and rejoiced in our victory.

A sudden sharp pain in my side caused me to wince. As my body jerked in reaction to the stinging sensation, a man's voice from behind me whispered, "Don't make a sound; walk slowly and don't do anything suspicious." I did not see the knife which he had concealed in a rolled-up newspaper but as he spoke I felt its point digging viciously into my side.

I did not know what was happening. One moment I was laughing and joking with my friends and the next there was a knife sticking in me. I wanted to scream, to cry out for help, but the shock and fear of what was happening stole my voice, leaving me terrified and speechless. Jabbing me with the blade, he put his face in front of mine and gestured with his head and eyes in the direction that he wanted me to walk.

It was a face I had seen before. Almost a month earlier, he and the rest of his family had been introduced to our congregation when some of his relatives had travelled and visited the church in which I was a member of the choir. Because of our family business – we owned gasoline stations, passenger jeeps for transportation and a welding shop – my mother was a wealthy woman and very well known in the district. His family would certainly have known about my mother, but we knew nothing about them. Apart from displaying the usual courtesy and manners required when new people were introduced to our area, I took absolutely no interest in him or his family. He was a twenty-seven-year-old man and I was a sixteen-year-old teenager and, like most sixteen-year-olds of that time, I was more interested in going outside to play with my friends.

Life in Lambajon was simple. Remote and far removed from any of the major cities, Davao city being the nearest and a good thirteen hours' drive away, life progressed there at a leisurely pace. As it was secluded and relatively untouched by outside influences, children and teenagers growing up there had an innocence that belied their years. Electricity had not reached Lambajon. If you were wealthy you had your own generator but most people used manpower to carry out everyday tasks and light in the evening was provided by kerosene-filled bottles and wicks.

School started at seven in the morning and finished at five in the evening, Monday to Friday. As it was already starting to get dark by five and with no street lighting, all of us school kids went straight from school to our houses. Once home, we did our homework, then did our chores around the house and found ways to amuse ourselves. For me, and because we were fortunate enough to be able to afford a generator, that would include singing karaoke or playing my guitar. There was no hanging around street corners – firstly, because there were no street corners, as all of the roads were either dirt tracks or filled with gravel; and secondly, because there was a curfew for kids under the age of twelve, which was enforceable after the hour of six o'clock, and one for adults that started from ten o'clock. If a child was found outside after this time without an adult accompanying them, they would be picked up by the police and brought back to their parents. The parents would be given a warning and a fine but if it happened again, the parents could be locked up for several days.

These conservative measures were in place because of the various rebel groups that inhabited the numerous mountainous regions and also because Lambajon was the base for the barracks of the Military Scout Rangers and the Military Airborne. Without ever being aware of it and because we knew no different, growing up there was a protected way of life.

Maybe that is why my body now froze with fear as this man terrorised me. With one arm around my shoulder and his other hand pressing the point of the knife menacingly into my side, he walked me hurriedly to the back gate and out of the school. The rear of the school was a very quiet area, planted with coconut trees and overgrown with high weeds. Because of the bad terrain and the poisonous snakes which inhabited that place, the road we walked was seldom used. As he walked me farther away from the school he suddenly took hold of my hair and pulled on it, jerking my head back roughly before putting his mouth to my ear. "If you try to run away from me I will kill you, I swear it," he said, pressing the knife even harder against my ribs.

I did not answer; I was crying and too scared to say anything to him. He never took his arm from around my shoulder or the knife from my side as he pulled me along with him and forced me to walk through the high weeds. My body was shaking and it seemed as though my feet were not touching the ground as he dragged me along. Overtaken by terror and fear, I closed my eyes, wanting to believe that blocking him out and denying what was happening would somehow make it stop. "Please God, I'm begging you, please don't let this man kill me, please take me back to my friends. I'm a good girl, I go to mass, I say my prayers, I respect my parents and I've never hurt anyone. Please save me, God, please!" Over and over I kept saying the words in my head, hoping that when I opened my eyes, like some miraculous charm they would send me back to where I had been, laughing and playing with my friends. But God was out of miracles that day.

I had no idea where we were going or why he was doing this to me but as we approached a small village called San Vicente, he squeezed me tighter to him and, once again putting his mouth to my ear, he whispered, "Remember and listen well: make a sound or try to run and you are dead." We walked into the small village and the few people we encountered paid no attention to us. They could not see the knife concealed in the newspaper and because of the way he was holding me with his arm around my shoulder, they obviously assumed that we were friends. When we came to a stop outside a house I had never seen before, he pushed me forward and said, "Go in." Once inside he dragged me by the hair into the kitchen and informed me that this was the house of his sister. I could not understand any of this and tried to gather myself. Why had he brought me to his sister's house? If he wanted to kill me it would have been a lot easier to do that in the wasteland that we had just trekked through than to do it here, where people had seen us enter the house. What did he and his sister want with me? But I did not get the opportunity to ask that question.

He was so much stronger than me. Placing his hands on my shoulders, he easily pushed me down onto one end of a long low-lying bench in the kitchen. Then, standing in front of me, he grabbed the back of my hair and viciously pulled my head back as he pressed the knife into my stomach, saying "Don't move." If he had applied even the smallest amount of extra force, that knife would have cut right into me. Out of pure instinct, I grabbed his hand to relieve the pressure on my stomach and pleaded with him through my tears, "Please stop this and let me go, please!" But my pleas for mercy only angered him. Like some demon from hell his face became horribly distorted as his eyes bulged and widened. I was looking into the face of the devil and it paralysed me with fear.

Unexpectedly he withdrew the knife from under my ribs and I prayed that he was letting me go but, like all my prayers that day, they went unanswered. He had only removed the knife so that he could draw back with his fist and punch me hard in the stomach, in the place where the knife had been. I had not been expecting the blow and the pain almost caused me to pass out. I felt my insides heave. With the wind punched out of me I gasped for air and once again I felt the point of the knife digging into my skin. "I am going to kill you, do you hear me?" he said, pushing his face menacingly into mine. I was going to die. Here, in a place where no one knew I had been taken and where my family would never find my body, I was going to meet my end.

He did not kill me but when he had finished with me I wished that he had. He held the knife close to my throat with one hand and with the other he reached under my majorette skirt, took hold of my underwear and violently ripped them from my body. I squeezed my thighs together and covered my nakedness with my hands. Screaming, I begged him to leave me alone. Taking absolutely no notice of my cries for mercy and acting as though I did not exist, he pushed me back onto the bench and mercilessly and repeatedly punched the inside of my thighs until, battered and numb, they finally fell open. Then, like the animal that he was, he penetrated me in an act of pure aggression, the burning pain becoming unbearable as he robbed me of my innocence and took my virginity in the horror of a brutal rape.

When he had finished with me and removed his body from mine, my hands went immediately between my thighs as if they could somehow hide my shame and soothe the sickening pain that was shooting through my body. But a new horror gripped me as my hands felt the wet blood that was pouring out of my brutalised vagina. I used my panties and skirt to try and stem the flow of blood. My body was in shock and I really thought I was going to bleed to death. I sat on the bench, shaking, not knowing what was going to happen to me.

Unbelievably, after subjecting me to this nightmare, this vile monster said, "I am sorry. I have been watching you for a long time now but I know your family will never accept me because you're rich and I am poor. But now, this is the way they will allow you to marry me."

Him, his words, everything about him disgusted me and all I could think about was how I could get away from this devil. Then, standing over and looking down on me as if I was now something that he owned, he continued, "I will call to your home tomorrow with my family and we will bring food and make arrangements for the wedding. Don't try to run away because if you do then I will find you and kill you and then I will burn down your house and your family's gasoline stations."

He had just finished making his threat when his sister and her husband arrived in the house. I knew by their smiles and the looks that my rapist exchanged with them that he was confirming that the deed had been done. They were all in on it. I had been set up by him and his family and they had all played a part in my premeditated rape.

I had to get out of there and away from them and that evil place. They did not resist when I ran to the door and out into the street. I was thankful for the fact that it was now dark and no one could see my tear-streaked face and blood-soaked dress as I ran all the way back home. I used the back door entrance to my home so no one could see me and went straight to my bedroom. Lying on the bed, my body aching and curled tightly into a ball, I tried to blot out the nightmare and the unbearable pain as I cried myself to a fitful sleep.

6

Lamb to the Slaughter

The following morning, I did not want to face anyone. I just wanted to stay in my room and lock myself away from the world and the monster who had left me feeling dirty and ashamed. I did not go down for breakfast and I did not go to school. My mother – who never had time for me when I was younger, choosing instead to spend all of her time in the business – was not aware of anything that had happened to me. I hadn't told her; I didn't know how and I was too ashamed.

My stepfather was not a man I could confide in either. He was a strict disciplinarian who would chastise me severely if he even so much as caught me looking in the direction of a boy. How could I tell him what had happened? Maybe he would think it was my fault, blame me and punish me.

So neither of them knew anything of what had happened until later that evening, when my rapist and his family arrived at our house.

"Come down here, Luz, you have visitors," my mom called up to my room.

The rapist and his family had arrived with food and drink. While my mother was surprised at the visit, my stepfather was absolutely furious that visitors had apparently been invited to our home without his permission. Again and again they called me, but I refused to go down. After a while my mother invited them in and my younger sister Fern, who was thirteen at the time, came running into my room.

"Our stepfather is very upset; the visitors are here to ask permission to marry you," she said, the surprise written all over her face.

"I don't care, Fern, tell them I am not going down there," was my reply, the anger now building inside me.

A while later my mother came into my room and on seeing me she asked, "Why are you crying, Luz? Why are you not going down to see your visitors? And why is this man asking to marry you? Do you know him?"

"No!" I snapped back at her.

"So if you don't know him, then why does he want to marry you?" she asked, puzzled.

"Because he raped me!" I spat out the answer through my tears.

There was silence for a moment and then she asked, "What did you just say?" as if disbelieving what her ears had just heard.

"Rape, Mom, that man downstairs, he *raped* me." I blurted out the reply with the words shaking in my throat.

I wanted so much to feel her arms around me, comforting and protecting me, and for her to tell me it was all going to be okay. But that did not happen. Even as a child, my mother seldom hugged me or showed me any real signs of affection. So from a very early age I had learned to care for and depend on no one but myself. Even after being brutally raped, it was more natural for me to keep it to myself than to look for comfort in the arms of my mother.

"Oh my God, you need to marry him before people start spreading rumours and causing embarrassment to our family," she said, shocked, but never once asking me if I was okay, or how it had happened, or even if I needed a doctor. She continued, "We really need to set your wedding up quickly so that there will be no gossiping about our family. You'd better come downstairs with me now before your stepfather throws them out." Her mind was working overtime. I knew that the embarrassment that could be caused to her because one of her daughters was no longer a virgin and could possibly be pregnant outside of marriage was of more concern than the fact that I had been raped.

"I don't care! He is not my boyfriend and I am not marrying him," I replied defiantly.

But my Mom was not taking "no" for an answer. With tears running down my cheeks and against my will, she marched me down the stairs and put me sitting next to the animal who had raped me only the day before. The rapist's parents were sitting at the table, as were his three brothers and three sisters.

When we were all sitting, my stepfather asked him, "Why are you here? What is your intention?"

The father of the rapist answered, "We are here because my son wants to marry your daughter."

"Do you love him?" my stepfather asked me, totally unaware that I had been raped.

I did not reply. I just sat there crying. Again my stepfather asked me, "Do you love him?" and once again I just continued crying. No one could see my abuser sticking his long nail in my side and pinching my skin as he sat by my side. I remembered his threat to kill me and to burn down our home and our business and I was too terrified to say anything.

His father started talking about the wedding and after about five minutes I went back to my bedroom. I checked my body where he had been pinching me; just above my hips I discovered an angry red mark about four inches long.

After a few minutes I was called downstairs to eat but I did not go. I stayed in my room, not wanting to hear a single word of their discussions. Downstairs my life was being discussed and dissected as if I did not exist. I was like some slaughtered piece of meat hanging on a hook in the market that was now being haggled over for the best price. Emotionally drained and physically exhausted by the pain in my body, I sat down and eventually fell asleep on my bed.

I stayed in my room the following morning. One of the house-helpers who noticed my absence brought the breakfast to my room. When she was leaving I asked her to send my sister up to me.

When Fern arrived I asked her what she had heard the previous night. She told me that there had been an argument over the date of the wedding and that later, when the visitors were gone, my stepfather and mother also had an argument. Fern had overheard my stepfather saying to my mother, "Why did you agree so quickly to this marriage? Why did you not speak with your daughter first?" Fern said he was really furious and that he also said, "So what if they come here with food and drink? They are the ones who ate and drank it. And anyway we didn't ask them to come here!" Fern said that my mother told him that it was not easy for them to have provided the food and that the marriage had to go ahead to avoid a scandal. My mother had chosen her moment wisely to tell him what had happened to me. My stepfather had a bad temper and she was scared at what he might do.

"I am not going to marry him, I hate him. I have a plan to escape; will you help me?" I asked Fern.

"Yes, of course I will. But what is your plan?" she asked.

The truth was that I didn't have a plan yet and it was not going to be easy to formulate one. Everyone in Lambajon knew me and our family and if they saw me in the jeep or leaving the area, they would be quick to let my mother know. I needed to think of something and I needed to be quick. The government departments in Baganga bought their gasoline from my mother and as a result she had lots of contacts in the municipal office. She used these contacts to push through the registration papers for the marriage, even though I was only sixteen years old and the rapist was twenty-seven.

Somehow my mother had learned from Fern that I was planning to run away and she confronted me over it. "If you have a plan to run away, don't do it. Everyone knows you are to be married now and you will cause a big embarrassment to our family. You need to attend your graduation and then prepare yourself for your wedding." She spoke without any thought or concern for how I was feeling.

"I don't care! I don't like him, I hate him, and even if I am pregnant from him raping me, I still won't marry him," I replied in defiance and self-defence.

My mother said nothing; but the following morning when I tried to open my bedroom door, I could not get it to budge. After a while I managed to force it open a little, just enough to see that my mother had tied a rope to the handle and attached the other end to the door across the hallway. I was horrified. She had made me a prisoner in my own home. She was happy to sacrifice me, her sixteen-year-old daughter, to my rapist so long as it meant she could maintain her standing in the community.

I had never had a close relationship with my mother but I had always tried to understand her and be an obedient daughter. I often reasoned that perhaps her own childhood had shaped her into the cold uncaring mother that I now knew. She was one of eight children and when she was just five years old, she witnessed her father, mother and eldest brother being massacred by Muslim rebels who attacked their house in Dao Capez City. My grandparents, my mother, two of her sisters and her brother were in the house at the time of the raid. On seeing the rebels approach the house, her elder sister Manang hid behind the curtain and my mother hid her younger sister under the dining-room table and covered her with the rice fan, a large circular mat used for selecting rice, before she rolled herself up inside a native mat. The rebels slashed and hacked her parents and brother to death before making off with the livestock and rice. It was a terrible thing to witness and to have to live through, but it could not excuse how she was treating me now.

I did not want to live any more. A bottle of rubbing alcohol in my room presented me with the opportunity to escape my prison and all of the horrors facing me. I drank it all then lay down on my bed and waited to die. One of the helpers who was tidying the room thought that I was having a nap but as she got closer to my bed she caught the smell of the rubbing alcohol from my breath and ran to get my mother. They arrived back in my room with coconut milk and sugar, which they mixed together, then held me down and forced me to drink it. After I had vomited the entire contents of my stomach, my mother chastised me and warned me not to do that again.

But I did not listen – I wanted to die. The rapist had taken more than my virginity; through this marriage he would rob me of my dreams. I had ambitions to be a military nurse or a flight stewardess, maybe even a singer, but now at just sixteen my dreams were gone.

I managed to get my hands on some tablets but they only had the effect of making me feel drunk.

As a protest against everything that was happening I took no willing part in any of the arrangements for the wedding. When it was time to go for a fitting for the wedding dress, I told them they could buy whatever dress they wanted, that I would not be going with them to choose or fit anything.

The morning of the wedding came and still I did not submit to anything that they had planned. The ceremony was arranged for ten o'clock that morning but by twelve o'clock I still had not shown up for it. Fifteen minutes later, the rapist showed up at the house looking for me. He was very upset because he thought I had run away. "Remember what I told you," he said, reminding me of his threat.

I arrived at the church at one o'clock, three hours late, but that made little difference; my mother had seen to that. The pastor was her cousin and he would be waiting at the church no matter how long it took for me to get there. All of this was wrong. It was evil and it seemed that God was sending signs to illustrate this fact. First, the bridesmaid ripped her dress on a chair as she walked up the aisle. Then as we were standing in front of the altar, a butterfly, which was very dark brown and black, landed on the shoulder of the rapist. Finally, on an otherwise glorious sunny day, during the ceremony the sky changed and we had a thunder and lightning storm.

During the entire ceremony I never opened my mouth. Even when the pastor asked if I would take him for my husband and if I loved him, I never answered. I was not going to give my consent to any part of this mockery. They might have forced my body to be there, but they would never force my heart.

When we were finished with the church we went back to his house, which was the tradition. There would be a party and his parents had set up a room in which we were supposed to consummate the marriage. I did not want to go to that house but I had no choice. My mother would ensure I arrived there one way or another. The party was in full swing when we got there and the music was being played at high volume through the sound system.

My new husband the rapist brought me into the bedroom and tried to kiss me but I pushed him away, repulsed by the very sight of him. He started shouting at the top of his voice as his face distorted grotesquely, just as it had done on that day when he so brutally raped me. I told him that I did not want him near me and that he had destroyed my life and every ambition that I had. Again he tried to kiss me and again I pushed him away, only this time he was ready for me. He grabbed my hand and twisted it back until I thought it was going to break; then with his other hand he delivered a sickening blow to my stomach. "Don't ever push me like that again, not unless you want to feel more of my fist," he growled as I crumpled and passed out in a heap on the floor. When I came around, my stomach was so sore and my thighs ached where they had been battered again. The man my mother had forced me to marry had just raped me again.

Lying on the floor, I turned my head to the side so as not to choke on my own vomit. I saw a knife hidden underneath the bedroom cabinet. Pulling myself up slowly and reaching under the cabinet, I retrieved the knife. Holding it in my hands, I felt shivers go down my spine as I recognised it as the knife that he had used when he raped me. I don't know where I got the strength but, with the knife in my hand, I went outside to where his mother and father were having breakfast. The rapist was in the underground cellar checking the coconuts. When his parents saw me, they said, "Come and join us for breakfast." I didn't answer but as I approached the table his mother asked, "What's that in your hands, Luz?"

Showing her the knife, I replied, "This is the knife your son used when he raped me and last night he beat me up and raped me again."

She cried when she looked at me. "He is your husband now, Luz, and only you and him can sort this out; but, just so that you know, not even his father can talk to him," she said wearily.

Whatever notions I might have held that his mother and father would somehow intervene and come to my rescue were now well and truly laid to rest. I went back to the house, put on a new dress and went to see my mom. I told her that I did not want to stay in his parents' house a moment longer. The marriage and the preserving of the family name was all that had interested her. She had got what she wanted and so, when I told her I wanted to get out of his parents' home, she bought the wood for my new house. Within three months it was built.

7

Reflections of Pain

The man I was married to was not only a rapist; he was also a sadist. Not once did he have sex with me without first beating me black-and-blue. More often than not I was unconscious by the time he started intercourse.

I needed to distract myself from what was happening to me. I asked my mother if I could enrol back in college, even if it was just a vocational course, and she said, "Why not?" Immediately I signed myself up for a secretarial course, which would take two years to complete. By day I worked as a cashier in the gasoline station and in the evening I attended the course. The rapist was working in forestry and he started work at half past five in the morning and did not finish until eight o'clock at night. This was good for me because by the time I would arrive home from the course he would be asleep and I would finally get some peace.

We didn't see each other for three days and I could almost fool myself into believing that my life was normal.

On the fourth night of the course, however, he unexpectedly finished work early and went straight to the college looking for me. When he arrived, I was standing in the corridor talking with two of my classmates while we waited for our next lesson to begin. I was not prepared for what he did next. In front of my classmates he grabbed me by the back of my hair and dragged me all the way to the house. I was embarrassed and felt so humiliated that he would treat me like that in front of my friends. When he got me inside the house, he screamed at me, "Who have you been with for the last three nights?" His eyes were filled with rage.

"Ah, so that's it – you're jealous!" I answered, glad that in some way I had been able to torment him, even if I had done it unwittingly. But he made me pay for my bravado with his fists. In a rage he delivered blow after blow to my stomach and mercifully I passed out from the pain.

The following day I told my mother about his jealousy but I did not tell her about his abuse. I was afraid that, if my stepfather found out, a big fight would break out between the two families and maybe someone would be killed. My mother told him to stop working in the forestry if it was going to be causing problems. She offered him a job as a conductor on one of her passenger jeeps, which he accepted. It meant he was always passing by the house when he needed gasoline and could keep a watch on me.

I fell pregnant but refused to give up my studies, so my mom sent me two helpers, which freed me from working in the house. I continued my job in the shop by day and pursued my studies by night.

One day my mom sent me to her cabinet to get a receipt book and while I was looking for it I came across two letters. One of them was addressed to me but had already been opened. It was from my husband the rapist; he had sent it to me before our wedding. In it he reiterated the threat he had made after he had raped me, which was that if I ran away then he would find me, kill me and burn down our home and business. The other letter was from my Auntie Nena, my mom's sister. She wrote, "They have to get married; you must protect the family." I did not tell my mom but I took the letter that was addressed to me and hid it away safely.

I was two months short of my due date when I experienced severe stomach pains and went prematurely into labour. On 4 February 1982 my daughter Charmie was born, weighing just four pounds exactly. She would spend three months in an incubator before I could take her home. I was just seventeen years old.

I was just two days over the labour and recovering when the animal that I was married to beat me up and raped me again, adding yet more horror to an already terrible existence.

When Charmie came home from the hospital, I had no feelings for her as a mother. I knew that she was a part of me, my own flesh and blood, but every time I looked at my own baby, I felt nothing but hate. Hate for the way she had been conceived in violence and rape. Hate for the way he had forced his seed, a part of a disgusting beast, to grow inside of me. And hate for the baby who was testament to every dirty, violent, sadistic and horrible thing he did to me.

I continued with my course; it was the only normal thing in my life and it provided a distraction which allowed me to function without going completely mad. My mother and the house-helper looked after and cared for Charmie. I didn't want her and I did not care if I never saw her.

With Charmie only six months old, I discovered that I was pregnant again. On 20 May 1983, I gave birth to my second child, Charlon, a boy. Like Charmie, he too was born two months premature and spent three months in an incubator. The birth and the baby meant nothing to me except getting rid of something from my body that was put there against my will. I was eighteen years old and the mother of two children.

After the birth of Charlon I did my best to avoid getting pregnant. The Philippines to this day is a predominantly Catholic country and in the 1980s, and particularly in a rural and very inaccessible place like Lambajon, contraceptives were just not available. If word got out that you were looking for contraceptives, you would be marked out as a woman of dubious character. So every morning I got up early to run, hoping that he would be gone to work by the time I got back, and at night I tried to sleep over in my mother's as much as possible.

One day when I was alone in my mom's and getting dressed, I caught sight of my naked body in the mirror and started to cry. The black, blue and yellow bruises that covered my stomach and thighs showed up so clearly in the light and I struggled to remember how my body looked without them. For two years now they had been viciously applied and reapplied to my body on an almost daily basis. As I saw my pitiful and battered reflection in the mirror I realised that the little girl in the majorette's uniform with a head full of wonderful dreams was gone and lost to me forever. I wondered what I had done in my life that was so bad that God had chosen to punish me like this. Why had he abandoned me, one of his children, and left me to suffer almost every day at the hands of a monster?

I missed my dad – my real father. He was a good and decent man and I knew that if he were still alive then none of this would have happened to me. My father's name was Alton Java. He was Chinese, born in the Philippines, and arrived in Baganga when he was just seventeen years old. It was not long before he opened a welding shop and it was so successful that within a few years he had his own garages and gasoline stations under the Caltex brand. He was a Southern Baptist and so devoted was he to his religion that he became a pastor and built the Southern Baptist church in our area. His love of music and singing was passed on to me and I remember fondly how, sitting on his knee, I would watch him as he wrote the notes to the music for the church choir.

He was much too young – only thirty-four years old – when he died. At age five I lost not only my father but my entire world. In his short lifetime, he had achieved so much and on his death my mother inherited thirty-six hectares of farm plantation used for growing abacá (a plant used for making very strong rope); four dump trucks; two motorcycles; two passenger jeeps; a welding shop; the Caltex gasoline stations; and of course our family home and whatever money my father had accumulated. Everyone was shocked when my father died so unexpectedly. He never smoked, he didn't drink and he was of very slight build and showed no signs of sickness.

He died on 11 February 1969 and by 28 December 1971, my mother was remarried to a Mr Johnny Ladroma, a house boy and one of the helpers, who was also my father's right-hand man. Less than seven months later on 13 July 1972, my mother gave birth to my half-brother Ricky. There were four children from the first marriage – my elder brother Alker, then me, followed by Fern my younger sister and Alton junior, my younger brother. The second marriage added two half-brothers to the family, first Ricky and then Ronnie.

Everything in our lives changed for the worse when my mother married that man. Not only was he a bully and a control freak but through his drinking, gambling and women, he would lose everything that my father had worked so hard to build up. My stepfather was a cruel man and if he was mad at us over something, he would not keep his temper in check. If we were late for dinner then it was much better that we hide and go hungry than show up and face his wrath because, after he was finished beating us, the only place we would not have bruises would be on our tongues. Other times he would beat us with his belt, burn the soles of our feet or fire live rounds around our feet with his gun.

My way of dealing with this man in our lives was to keep myself as busy as possible and in that way I would not have to think about him. I got involved in athletics and every morning at five o'clock I got out of bed and completed one hour's training before I went to school. I was so fed up having to beg to my mom and stepfather every time I needed even the most basic of things that I started making my own ice candy and sold it in my school, making my own money.

My other passion was singing. When I was eleven years old news reached me that there was a competition as part of the fiesta activities, with a prize of one hundred and fifty peso for the winner, it was too good an opportunity to miss. My mom or my stepfather would never let me join the competition so I entered in secret. I was selling my ice candy at the event, so my mom was not suspicious of me being in that area with her. I wish I had a picture of the look of horror and embarrassment on her face when I was announced and walked out onto the stage to sing as one of the finalists in the competition! My mom hid behind a pillar the whole time that I was singing and when I left the stage she asked me, "Are you not embarrassed for yourself and our whole family, singing like that?"

"No, why should I be embarrassed, mom? If anyone thinks they can do better, then let them get up on the stage and sing! At least I tried," I replied, upset that she could not be proud of me for being a finalist. While we were talking, the master of ceremonies announced the winner – it was me! I was so delighted to have won but more importantly I learned a valuable lesson that day: never in my life would I let anyone tell me what I could or could not achieve. For certain there would be times I would fail, but it would never be for the lack of trying.

One day I saw my stepfather, the man who was so strict with all of us, giving money to a woman I had never seen before. When I arrived back at the house I told my mom what I had seen. I had no idea that this was some other woman he had on the side. My mom had an almighty row with him when he came home and in the height of a temper he came looking for me. When he found me, he grabbed me roughly by the hair and started shaking me.

That was the way that he was and I blame my mother for everything that happened to us. She stood back while he physically abused and terrorised her children and she watched and did nothing while he gambled, drank and womanised our livelihood away.

These memories stirred something within me and as I looked in the mirror at my bruised and violated body I swore that no one would ever do that to me again.

Innocence lost was now replaced by a fire that was igniting in my belly.

8

Lioness

"Jesus Christ, who did that to you, Luz?" my neighbour Andrea cried out in horror as I lifted my dress and revealed for the first time to anyone the bruises that adorned my body.

Andrea was in her late forties. She was a kind and gentle woman and her daughter Vivian and I were the best of friends. I went on to explain to Andrea how I was being abused by the animal that was my husband and that I was confiding in and trusting her because I needed help to escape and run away from him. "Why have you not shown and told all of this to your mom, Luz?" she asked, shocked by what I had told her.

"If my mom had not forced me to marry him in the first place then none of this would be happening," I replied, unable to conceal the hatred I felt for my mother and what she had done. "And if some of my family see and hear about this, Andrea, maybe they will kill him and then I will not only have his blood on my hands but I will have to live the rest of my life knowing that as well as abusing me, he had also, because of me, turned one of my family into a criminal. That is just too high a price to pay." I hoped she could understand the dilemma I faced.

"God bless you, kid, you are too young to be suffering like that. Of course I will help you if I can," she said, hugging me tightly. She advised me to pack a bag and hide it somewhere safe so that when the opportunity came for me to run, I would be ready. I knew I would have to be patient, as he was always around, and even if I managed to run, I would have to ensure that I had time enough to put as much distance as possible between him and me or else he would be able to track me down.

I tried to pretend that everything was going along as normal, but there was no pretending about the sick feeling in my stomach, which had caused me to vomit on two consecutive mornings. I knew, despite my denials and trying to convince myself to the contrary, that I was pregnant again. I was distraught. Another year brought another pregnancy that I simply did not want. Every time I gave birth, I did not see a baby; all that I saw and knew was that I had produced another link in an unbreakable chain that would bind me and my life to that rapist and sadist forever.

Pregnant or not, nothing was stopping me from my plan to escape; for if I did not get away from him now, I never would.

One of my mom's helpers had a daughter who was getting married and the wedding day provided a welcome distraction from all that was going on inside my head.

Thankfully because of his work commitments my husband the rapist could not attend the wedding. It meant that I could relax and enjoy myself; I could smile and actually breathe at the reception without him watching my every move and suffocating me. I was laughing and really enjoying the party and the company of the bride and groom who, along with their parents, were sharing the same table as my mom and me.

But the laughter was short-lived. From out of nowhere I saw my husband coming towards me, a look of pure evil and menace on his face. He was so jealous and possessive that he had skipped off work to check on me and to see what I was up to. The sight of me actually enjoying myself and laughing with other people tipped him over the edge. When he got to where I was sitting and in full view of everyone, he grabbed me – his pregnant wife – by the hair, pulled me up from the table and dragged me all the way home. When he got me inside the house, without any warning he drew back with his fist and smashed me in the face, almost breaking my jaw. The blow stunned me and sent me reeling backwards, but he had gone too far.

I had sworn I would not let him abuse me again and so the mouse became a lioness. Grabbing the machete that was lying on the table I swung it with all my might, aiming the blow at his head. He instinctively pulled back, but not quickly enough. Before he could get his head out of the way, the machete slashed through the towel that was about his neck and it turned deep red as the blood started to flow profusely from the wound in his flesh. The sight of the blood terrified me; I dropped the machete from my hands and ran as fast as I could to the back of the house.

Just then my mom and stepfather arrived. My mother had told my stepfather what had happened and now he was standing in the house brandishing an M16 assault rifle and he shot up the ground beneath my husband the rapist's feet with a hail of bullets, threatening to kill him. With my stepfather still firing rounds at him, he ran out of the house and went into hiding.

It was a terrifying sequence of events, but although I was shaking and in a lot of pain from the blow to my chin, I knew that this was my moment to escape. He would be too afraid to come back to the house that night in case my stepfather was waiting for him, so this would give me the head-start I needed before he noticed I was gone and came looking for me. It was now or never. I knew that Charlon and Charmie would be okay with my mother and her helpers and I dared not tell my mom what I was planning to do in case she tried to stop me.

I was nineteen years old and, with just a small bag packed with some items of clothing and a little food, pregnant with my third child and without any idea of where I was going, I turned my back on Lambajon Baganga, my family and my children and walked without fear into the dark of the night.

As I looked back over my shoulder to the place where I had been humiliated, beaten and brutalised in ways that left me feeling less than human, I smiled. For however black and foreboding the night that lay ahead, it would pale in comparison to the dark and evil soul of the monster I was leaving behind.

9

Life and Death

San Juan village in Agdao, Davao, is a good thirteen
hours' journey by passenger jeep from Baganga. It entails
a gruelling eight-hour drive on a twisting, winding dirt
road that takes you to Mati and the highway and then
onto a smoother five-hour drive to Davao City. It was
because of the distance it would put between me and my
husband, and the fact that two of my father's brothers –
my uncle Ely and my uncle Dixie – lived there that I made
Davao my destination. I knew I could count on my uncles
to take me in. I arrived in Davao City at twelve noon,
exhausted by the previous day's events but elated at
having got this far. Perhaps now I would finally have
some peace in my life. I was four months pregnant at this
time, and I decided that I would stay there at least until
my baby was born.

Davao was going through a major period of political
upheaval at this time with rebel groups in constant

conflict with government troops and different vigilante groups dealing out their own versions of justice. It is fair to say that at this time Davao was the most lawless city in the Philippines, as well as being one of the biggest cities in the world.

As I entered San Juan village, Agdao, and approached my uncle's house, I had no idea that I was in the midst of one of the most notorious of these groups, called "Sparrow". As expected, my uncles and their families welcomed me with open arms. It was so nice sitting with them over dinner as we swapped our stories. An unexpected knock on the door interrupted our chat and my uncle got up from the table to see who it was. I could hear him inviting someone into the house and when he returned to the table there was another man with him. This man took a gun from his pocket and placed it on the table. He pointed at me and asked my uncle and my aunt, "Who is she, what is she doing here and where is she from?" All strangers entering the area were considered potential spies and I was no exception.

If the gun was meant to scare me, it did not succeed. My stepfather was leader of the Civilian Head Defence Force (CHDF) in Lambajon and I had grown up with rifles, handguns and all sorts of firearms, including grenades, as part of my everyday life. What did bother me, though, was that I'd had no idea just how critical this area was and I knew that a stray bullet could have anyone's name on it.

One day my auntie suggested that we should go and do some shopping in the market in Agdao. You need to travel there by jeepney, which is a type of mini-bus. We walked to the terminus and joined the queue. You enter a jeepney one at a time from a small opening in the back. When it arrived, my auntie was the first to board it and I followed her, standing in the doorway and holding onto one of the safety handles at either side of the entrance. On noticing that I was pregnant, a man who was also standing in the doorway beckoned me to enter the jeepney before him. I accepted his polite gesture and with one foot in the jeepney and the other still planted on the ground, I turned my head to look back at him, to thank him for his good manners. I was surprised when I looked back because, with my words of thanks already halfway out of my mouth, I realised he was not standing where he should have been. Instead he was lying face down on the ground with the blood pumping out of a hole in the back of his neck where a bullet had entered it and killed him.

It was the first time I had been so close to someone who had been shot and killed. My body started shaking uncontrollably with the realisation that it could just as easily have been me face down in the dirt. When we got to the market my auntie calmed me down, saying, "That's the way it is here now, Luz. After a while you just get used to it."

Every day the killings continued. Even if you were just going about your own business, you never knew when you might just get caught up in the middle of a shooting. One night I was in my uncle Dixie's house watching a film on TV with his family when someone shouted into us from outside in the street, "Turn out the lights, turn out the lights!" We turned off the lights and everyone ducked and lay flat out on the floor. Then we heard the gunshots, *bang–bang–bang*, three times they fired, and then silence. After about five minutes we picked ourselves up from the floor and looked outside. All of the neighbours were running out of their houses and gathering outside my uncle's house. The man who, only a few minutes earlier, had shouted in to us was in a heap on the ground, shot dead with the three bullets in him.

Despite what my auntie had said to me that day in Agdao market, I would never get used to this killing. We tried to live our lives as normally as possible but there was nothing normal about being surrounded by all of this death.

At three o'clock in the afternoon of 26 April 1985, in the midst of all this carnage, I brought a new life into the world when I gave birth to my third child, a baby boy. I named him Richard.

A few days prior to Richard's birth, news had filtered into Agdao that the Military Airborne Scout Rangers were preparing a raid on the village in an attempt to take out the Sparrow unit. This had the potential to be a very bloody confrontation. No one knew for sure when the raid was planned; it could happen any time. But it did not happen just any time – it happened just hours after I had given birth to my baby and while I was still recovering from the labour in my uncle Ely's house.

It was eight o'clock in the night and the sudden outbreak of repeated gunfire shattered the silence of an otherwise peaceful night. As I swung my legs out of the bed and made my way to the window to see what was happening, I knew that the threatened raid had begun.

With the intensity of the gunfire increasing and drawing ever closer to our position, I feared for my life and the life of my newborn baby. I had to get out of there and so hurriedly I threw on some clothes and, wrapping my baby in a blanket and accompanied by my cousin, I fled the house through the back door. I did not stop running until we came to the wall that marked the boundary of the village. The wall was approximately six feet high and together we scaled it, passing Richard to each other as we took it in turns to make the climb.

Once on the other side of the wall we found ourselves on the grounds of a factory called Main Trade. With the gunfire still raging about us and the military guarding the roads in and out of the village, it was far too risky and dangerous to travel over ground. There was only one other alternative and so, only hours after giving birth and, holding my baby high, we plunged into the open end of the sewer that led away from the village and waded neck-high through the filthy waste.

Rats and sewers are a match made in hell, an unholy alliance forged to produce fear and dread. I made my way slowly and silently through the sewer, filled with the stench of human waste, holding Richard high above my head. I feared for my life as I dreaded how this rat-infested sludge could be infecting my body, a body that was particularly vulnerable having only just given birth. Several times I lost my footing on the uneven surface beneath my feet and I clenched my teeth and squeezed my mouth shut as my head plunged into the filth. Each time it happened I spluttered and choked, adding my own vomit to the already vile contents of this cesspool. I could not afford to stumble and fall, for if I did and Richard was to sink below the filthy waste, it would almost certainly mean death for him.

Whenever I came across a clearing in the bank, I took the opportunity to place Richard on the bank's edge and rest my aching arms. I used whatever foliage was available along the bank to clean my face of the dirt that had stuck to it and rubbed my hands in the weeds to clean them as best I could, afraid to use Richard's blanket for fear of contaminating him with this filth. All around me I could hear the movement of rats and insects moving through the undergrowth, and hastily I took Richard back in my hands and continued on our escape. My cousin suggested that we take it in turns to carry Richard, but I was not prepared to entrust his life to anyone else. I had come too far and suffered too much to lose him now.

The trauma of the birth and the day's events began to take effect. I was exhausted. The energy was leaving my body and all I wanted to do was lie down and rest, but I had to keep going. "Come on, Luz, you have survived worse than this! Now is not the time to lay down and die." I kept chanting the words over and over to myself as I dug deeper to find the strength to continue. Richard's father was a monster. He had tried to dehumanise me, to break my spirit and condemn me to a life of misery. I hated him and now I focused on that hate and used it to spur me on. I recalled every vile word from his mouth and felt every hurt he inflicted on my body and channelled the anger it provoked into a determination to survive. I would survive for my children, for the baby in my arms, and make something of my life, even if it was just to spite him.

It worked. Lost in and motivated by my hate, I had ignored the pain and overcome my exhaustion, only snapping out of this trance-like state when my cousin excitedly said, "Look, Luz, lights! We have reached the end."

We had travelled through the sewer for about thirty gruelling minutes, coming to stop at a place called Salmonan. Once there, we knew it was safe to leave the sewer and continue our journey over land. We hauled our tired, wet, stinking and exhausted bodies from the filthy waste and travelled another thirty minutes by foot until we came to the subdivision of Dacobel and the home of my cousin Bebe, the daughter of my mom's sister.

We stayed with Bebe and her husband for two weeks, by which time we were joined there by my uncle Ely and his family. The two weeks were a welcome opportunity to rest and recover my strength and a rare chance for me to reflect on the course of my crazy life.

I nursed Richard. Charmie and Charlon had been bottle-fed, as I simply did not want them anywhere near me, but with Richard I bonded with my baby and for the first time I felt like and accepted that I was a *mother*. Maybe it was because I had no choice. There was no one to hand my baby over to and I knew his survival depended on my care. Yet I knew it was more than that. I had given birth to Richard far away from the reach of the animal who had fathered him, and in some way that distance removed the association of him with this baby. When I looked at Richard I saw *my* baby and not an *object* or a thing that was a forerunner to the other *things*

I would be *forced* to produce. That threat was gone. I would never be forced again. I did not have to wait for the moment when he would burst into my room and rape me and force me to *produce* a part of him again. Richard represented my escape from that world of violence and abuse.

While I had been in San Juan, Agdao, my mother used to visit once a month and bring me some money to support myself. She would also bring Charmie and Charlon to visit me, but I never spent even a minute with them. In my mind, to accept them was to accept what had been done to me. I hated what had been done to me and I was never going to accept it. Even with Richard arousing my motherly instincts, I still could not break down that wall of hate.

Although we were grateful for the hospitality shown to us by Bebe and her husband, we could not impose on them any longer. My grandpa's house in M'lang, North Cotabato, was a four-hour drive from Dacobel. When he had died it was inherited by my father and he had allowed the tenants to stay there rent-free as long as they maintained the property and cared for the land. It seemed the logical place to go.

We had only been there a few days when we realised that we had jumped out of the frying pan and into the fire. None of us had realised just how dangerous this area was, with constant fighting taking place between Christian and Muslim factions. Just being there was enough in itself to make you a legitimate target for whoever fancied taking a shot at you. However, we were walking about with targets on our heads when I discovered that my uncle Norberto

Manero, my godfather, was also the infamous Commander Bukay, leader of the anti-communist group called "Ilaga Vigilantes" – Ilaga meaning rat. He had a fearsome reputation and on 11 April of that year, fifteen days before my son Richard had been born, he had killed Father Tulio Favali, a missionary priest with the Pontifical Institute for Foreign Missions, accusing him of being a communist sympathiser. He would later pay for that crime by spending twenty-two years of his life in prison but at this time he was still at large. Rumours were rife that Norberto was a cannibal and that he had eaten the brains of the dead priest. Whatever the truth of that story, one thing was certain: he was a man to be feared.

His brothers, Edelberto and Elpido Manero, were also members of the Ilaga Vigilantes and every bit as fearsome as their brother. They were, of course, marked men. The nature of their lives meant that they had made many enemies and revenge attacks were always expected.

Until we had arrived there, I had no idea about any of this. The downside for me and Richard was that now, because we were being visited in the house by my godfather and his group, we would also be viewed as legitimate targets for his enemies.

When I told my godfather and his nephew, my cousin Crispin, who was also a member of the Ilaga group, about how I had suffered at the hands of my husband the rapist, they went wild and wanted to kill him. After what he had done to me it would have been welcome justice, but the fact remained that he was the father of my children and I was not going to be the cause of them being fatherless. They thought I was crazy for thinking like this but they respected my decision. "You have to make yourself strong, Luz, so that no one will ever do that to you again," they said. They began a regime of training to teach me self-defence and fighting techniques.

It was good that I learned to be strong and defend myself, but of equal importance for me and Richard was that I needed to find a way to support myself financially. Getting rice was not a problem. The tenants who were living freely on the land gave us all the rice that we needed and for all our other needs I opened a small grocery shop at the front of the house. But with the situation in M'lang getting more critical by the day and after spending three months in North Cotabato, I made the decision to travel to South Cotabato in search of a more peaceful life for me and my baby.

My elder brother Alker and another of my father's brothers, uncle Charlie, lived in Polomolok, South Cotabato, so at least I would have family there to support me while I tried to carve out a life for myself and get back on my feet. As things had quietened in Davao, my uncle Ely and his family returned to their home in San Juan, Agdao. In July 1985 I arrived with Richard in Cannery, Polomolok, South Cotabato and moved into an apartment with my brother Alker and his wife Adela. It was so good to get some peace finally and to be able to sleep at night with both eyes closed, rather than having to keep one open in case someone broke in to kill you.

I immediately set about looking for work. I liked to be independent and with Richard to provide for, I had no time to waste. The huge Dole pineapple plantation is situated in Polomolok. It is a big provider of employment in that area and with one of my father's five brothers, my uncle Frank, working there as the hiring officer, it seemed to me to be as good a place as any to start on my quest for work.

Unfortunately, when I asked my uncle Frank for a job, he said, "Sorry, we have no vacancies – only planting positions available for men."

"I don't care what job I have to do. I have a baby to feed, so just give me a chance, that's all I'm asking from you," I pleaded with him.

"But we have never had women planters here," he replied, a little taken aback by my determination. "Anyway, maybe you aren't strong enough for the work and can't do it even if I give you the job."

"If I can't, then I can't. But what have you got to lose by just letting me try?"

I got the job. I was the first woman planter to be hired by Dole and I started that very same day. My uncle had been right; that first day was so hard. The work involved spending most of the day bent over, firstly to spread the markers and pineapple crowns for planting, and then again to plant them. But I learned that day how to do the work and I completed it.

The next morning I awoke at three o'clock in agony. Every part of my body ached and I was running a very high temperature. I had overestimated my strength, failing to take into account the fact that, since giving birth to Richard, I had not had a moment's rest. But knowing what was wrong would not feed me or my baby. I needed that job and, through pure will and determination, I somehow managed to drag myself out of that bed and into the shower. I let the water pour over me and, as it eased the pain a little, my mind started thinking of ways to make this job easier.

I made sure I arrived at the plantation with plenty of time to spare and used it to study the techniques used for the planting. So much time was wasted by spreading and then clearing unnecessary markers that it made the job more difficult and time-consuming than it had to be. Armed with this knowledge, I devised a technique whereby I could carry the pineapple crowns in a basket over my head and then spread the markers only where I needed them.

The result of my new technique was that on pay day I received three cheques – one for my salary, the other two being bonuses for achieving and surpassing my incentives. I was the first woman to achieve this and using my technique I was planting on average around 15,000 crowns a day.

10

The Long Goodbye

Noel

At first I had listened to Luz completely spellbound and captivated by her tale. Now I was not just listening, I was looking at her in awe and total admiration not only for what she had survived but also for what she had achieved and the seemingly insurmountable odds and challenges over which she had triumphed.

"Well, that's part one of my story, Noel. I hope it hasn't bored you too much," she said, smiling at me, knowing perfectly well that she had been anything but boring.

"Part one, Luz? You mean there's more?" I replied in disbelief and thinking, *surely not!*

"I'm afraid that there is, Noel, a lot more, and it gets even more complicated," she replied. I sensed that she was enjoying the look of surprise in my eyes. "Shall I continue?"

Although Luz was smiling and I was really intrigued to hear the rest of her tale, I noticed that it had been draining on her emotionally, such was the honesty and frankness of her account. I needed to bring some levity to our chat and give her time to recover.

"I'd love to hear the rest of your story, Luz, but perhaps I need a little time to digest everything you've told me. There's so much to take in," I replied, hoping that she would not misinterpret my concern as lack of interest. Quickly I added, "I don't know about you, Luz, and perhaps I'm pushing my luck, but it's ages since I've been to the cinema. Since you paid for the coffee, would you like to go to a movie with me as my treat? The cinema's just around the corner from here."

I tried to look casual as I stood up and took her jacket from the chair, holding it open for her to put on, but inside my stomach was doing somersaults as I waited for her reply.

"Yes, why not?" she said. "I love the cinema and it will be good to chill out."

If you were to ask me the name of that film I can give you the answer instantly: *About Schmidt*, starring Jack Nicholson and Kathy Bates. But if you were to ask me what the film was about, I wouldn't have a clue. From the moment we took our seats until the final credits scrolled up the screen, one part of my brain was trying to make sense of the unlikely set of events that had just unfolded while the other half was appreciating this beautiful and incredible woman sitting beside me. I was inexplicably drawn to her and I wanted so much to hug her, to offer her not sympathy but comfort and understanding for all that had happened in her life. But as much as I was feeling rejuvenated and assertive that day, I had not gone completely mad. I knew all too well that a black eye takes a long time to heal.

Several times through the course of the movie we caught each other taking sly glances from the corners of our eyes as we both tried to weigh up what the other was thinking. When the movie was over and without really thinking about it, we headed back towards the hotel. "Luz, let's go in and have another coffee and you can tell me the rest of your story," I said, not wanting our time together to come to an end.

"Okay, let's have the coffee, Noel, but maybe the story will have to wait for another day. I've already made arrangements to meet some friends for dinner and it's almost time that I made my way to them," she replied, looking at her watch.

As we walked into the hotel I had mixed feelings. I was sad that our time together was coming to an end but happy and relieved that, as we walked back into the hotel, with less than twenty euro left from the forty I had started out with that day, I would not have to embarrass myself and find an excuse for why I could not buy dinner. We chatted some more over the coffee and sandwiches.

Luz's mobile rang; it was her friends looking for her. Luz had told me they were a couple whom she had helped out with a work problem and that they had invited her to dinner by way of thanks. The girl, Ruby, was Filipina and Luz had known her a long time. Her husband Naufel was from India. "Okay, I will be there in a while, Ruby," Luz said, raising her eyebrows and indicating to me that she really had to go.

In jest, I said to Luz, "Tell them it's no problem – sure you can just bring me with you!"

I could not believe my ears when Luz, having taken my quip quite literally, said, "Do you mind if I bring a friend along with me, Ruby?" I was speechless but delighted that this day was not over yet.

We joined Ruby and Naufel in Yamamori, a restaurant in George's Street. Luz introduced me simply as "my friend". During the course of the meal we chatted mostly about Ruby and Naufel and their work status here in Ireland. As I chased a piece of sushi around the plate with the unfamiliar chopsticks, wondering if I should just spear the slippery little bugger with the stick instead of trying to pinch it between these two torturous pieces of wood, the hilarity of the whole scenario hit me. Here I was, Noel from Dublin, sitting in a Japanese restaurant eating sushi and drinking saké with two Filipinas and a guy from India, all of whom I had met within the space of a few short hours. I had wanted this day to be different and I was certainly getting what I asked for.

We finished the meal about nine o'clock that night and the four of us chatted as we walked towards the quays. Naufel and Ruby said their goodbyes, leaving Luz and me once again on our own.

"That was very enjoyable, Luz. They seem like really nice people," I said as we watched them wave goodbye from the far side of the road.

"Yes, it was, and they are," Luz replied, closing her jacket against the cold of the night.

We walked a little farther down the quays until we reached a bus stop. Luz said, "Well, Noel, this is my bus stop. I think it's about time I headed back home. How about you? Where are you off to next?"

I didn't want her to go and I couldn't fully understand why. What was happening to me was so totally unexpected, but it felt as though I had known this woman all of my life. If someone had been able to see into my mind and heart and extract from them my ideal of the perfect woman and then somehow make her manifest in front of me, I would be looking at Luz. It was too scary and I wondered if maybe I was going mad again. Or was someone playing with my mind? Was all of this simply a dream from which I would suddenly and painfully wake? Well, if it was all or any of those things, then this madman would happily remain in this sleep forever.

"Next? Oh, I've nothing planned, Luz – except to get on a bus with this lovely lady I met today and make sure she gets back home safely," I replied, hoping to gain some more time before I had to let her go.

"Well, if you're sure it's not too much trouble, Noel, that would be really nice," she laughed. From the way she smiled, I sensed that it was not just me who did not want this night to end.

Luz's apartment was situated on Conyngham Road, opposite the Phoenix Park and only a short bus ride away. When we arrived there Luz invited me in for tea. As Luz filled the kettle and made a snack, I sat on the sofa and took in the apartment. It was small but very compact and everything in it was beautifully put together. With the tea and the snack made, Luz came over and joined me on the sofa.

"If you feel up to it, Luz, I would really love to hear the rest of your story," I said, accepting a mug of tea.

"Are you sure, Noel? It's ten-thirty now and perhaps you'll have to get home soon."

"Not at all, Luz – how could I possibly go now, knowing only half of your incredible tale? Please go on from where we left off in the hotel. I'm all ears."

Smiling, Luz said, "Okay, Noel, where were we?"

11

Kidnapped

Luz

Having secured the job with the Dole plantation, I was now earning a decent living. It was hard work, there was no denying that, but now I could easily provide for Richard and me and life was starting to feel good again. I had not forgotten the evil monster I had left behind or the terrible things he had subjected me to. Although his brutality might remain in my mind forever, at least the bruises on the outside were gone. I looked at myself in the mirror and I cried tears of happiness. For the first time in a long, long time I could look at my reflection and not feel disgusted by what I saw. I could even begin to imagine that I was pretty and enjoy how it felt to be human again.

I had a few admirers when I was working in the Dole plantation. They would often ask me out on dates but because of what I had already experienced at the hands of a man and with the memories of what he had done to me still very clear, I had no interest in these men or any man and always refused their advances. I was enjoying being me and being just me meant I was free!

The newspaper dropped from my hands. As I felt the blood drain from my head, I slumped into the chair and cried out, "*No!*"

He was looking for me; the evil sadistic bastard was looking for me. He had put my picture in the paper, asking for anyone who saw me to get in contact with him. Just when I had managed to make a life, had begun to taste freedom and enjoy not living in fear, his vile hands were once again reaching out, trying to take hold of me. Perhaps I should have taken up my uncle's and my cousin's offer to kill him; at least then I would not be living in fear of him now.

He could come looking if he wanted but I was not going to run any more. I had made a life for myself and Richard here in Polomolok. Nothing or no one was going to take it away from me. I had worked and sweated too hard to allow that to happen. Now that I was aware he was still looking for me, I could be on my guard and be somewhat prepared if he showed up.

In July 1985, a singing contest as part of the fiesta celebrations in Polomolok was too much temptation for me to resist. Apart from the joy of singing on stage, the prize money would always be very welcome. I won the competition and was making my way off the stage, having collected my prize, when a man grabbed my hand, shook it and said, "Well done! I am Mr Morales."

I took little notice of him, politely said "Thanks," and went on my way.

One day at work I saw him again; he was working in Dole, but for a private company driving a spraying tanker. When he saw me he came over, reintroduced himself and asked, "Can I visit you in your house?"

I immediately replied, "I don't have a house, and why do you want to visit me anyway even if I did? Do I look sick?"

He smiled and said okay; but every day after that he kept bothering me at work, asking me to allow him to visit. I felt no attraction to him and rebuffed his advances as politely as possible. Hopefully he would get the message and leave me alone.

It was now 1986 and Richard was one year old. I needed to buy some things and for a change I thought I would head to Davao City to do my shopping. Because of my work I did not get much time to spend with Richard and so, despite the fact that it was a long four-hour bus journey, I took him with me. The bus to Davao terminates beside a church and every time I went there I would always go in for at least a few minutes to say some prayers. This time, as I entered I met a distant relative of mine called Emily. She invited me back to her house, where we continued our chat and caught up on what was happening in our lives.

I hadn't realised how much time had passed since we started talking. With Richard already asleep, tired out from the journey, I asked Emily if she would look after him for an hour or so while I dashed around the shops before they closed. Emily was delighted to oblige and told me to go and take as much time as I needed. She told her two boys, who were six and eleven years old, to be quiet and let Richard enjoy his sleep. Without having to carry Richard around with me I would get around the shops much more quickly, giving myself plenty of time to catch the bus back home.

With my shopping completed I arrived back at Emily's house but was surprised when nobody answered the door. *Maybe they have gone for a sleep*, I thought, so I called out Emily's name as I banged on the door, but still there was no reply. *Ah, they must have gone for a walk with Richard*, was my next thought. So I sat at the front of the house and waited for them to return. I waited and waited for more than two hours and still there was no sign of them.

I was not overly worried about Richard at this time. I knew he was with Emily, wherever she was, but as it was already dark, and the last bus for Polomolok was leaving shortly, I was worried that I might miss it. If I missed that bus I would not be able to get back home and show for work the following morning; if that happened I would lose my job. I knocked on the doors of some of the neighbours' houses in case they might have seen Emily go out and knew where she was, but none of them had seen her.

I had to make a decision: stay and lose my job or come back in the morning and collect Richard. There was really no choice. I needed that job to provide for Richard and myself. Emily could not be contacted by phone, as mobile phones were not available at the time and only very wealthy people possessed a land line. It was so frustrating. So I left word with the neighbours to tell Emily when she got back home that I would return tomorrow to collect Richard from her.

I reported to my supervisor the next day and when I explained to him what had happened, he allowed me the day off to travel back to Davao to collect Richard. But when I got to Emily's house there was still no sign of her or Richard and none of the neighbours had seen Emily either. I spent the whole day outside the house, waiting for her to return, but she never showed up.

All sorts of things were now going through my head. Although I knew that I should be getting worried, I fooled myself into believing that there would be a simple and innocent explanation for all of this. The alternative was too frightening to consider. I waited at Emily's house for as long as I could, until the last bus back to Polomolok pulled into the station to take me home.

I could not sleep. Anxiety had taken hold and I spent a restless night, upset and confused, wishing for the morning to arrive so I could go back to Emily's to find Richard. When it did I once again asked my supervisor for time off so I could go to look for my son and thankfully he agreed.

When I got to Emily's house, there was still no sign of her. Now the panic and fear set in. Where could they be? Where was my baby? Why did nobody know where Emily was? I had not brought any food or a change of clothes for Richard when I had left him with Emily and I fought back the tears as I worried how he was being cared for.

I walked the streets of Bunawan, the area in Davao City where Emily lived, searching frantically for her and

Richard and asking everyone I encountered if they had seen them, but the answer was always the same: *No!*

Daylight was again fading fast and it was almost time to get the last bus back to Polomolok but before I did I would pass by Emily's house one more time. The house was still vacant. As I turned away, dejected and exhausted, I was surprised by a voice behind me. "Don't be worrying yourself, dear, just think about it for a minute. This is Emily's home; she has to return here sometime and when she does I am sure it will all be okay." The voice belonged to an old woman I had spoken to earlier that day.

She was right. Emily would not abandon her home. She would have to return and no matter how long that took I would be waiting for her when she did. I thanked the old woman for her words of encouragement before hurrying to the station for my bus home.

When I arrived back in Polomolok I discussed the day's events with my eldest brother Alker, but he just dismissed all my fears and concerns, saying, "Why are you worrying, Luz? Emily is family and I am sure there is a very good explanation as to why she suddenly had to go away." Neither my brother nor his wife Adela seemed to be the least bit concerned. Their conviction that everything was okay, when combined with the words of the old woman I had spoken to earlier, helped to put my mind a little more at ease.

Of course, every instinct was telling me to go to the police, but if I did that, I would be signing my own death warrant. You see, not only had my husband the rapist posted a notice in the newspapers along with my picture in his search for me; he had also posted my picture in many of the police stations and areas in which I was known. The moment I stepped inside a police station and mentioned my name and Richard's family name, I would be as good as back in my husband's evil clutches. There would be no point in me trying to plead my case to the police – in their eyes I would be seen as my husband's property and for them it would be as simple as that. I would be held until he came to collect me and there would be nothing I could do about it. Then, and in order for him to save face from the embarrassment I caused him by running away, I would be dragged home so that everyone could see he had me again, and then I would be raped and brutalised so he could enforce his ownership of me. I would kill myself before I let that happen.

I could not ask for any more time off work. Jobs with the Dole pineapple plantation were highly prized and there was always someone else who would be only too willing to step in and fill my shoes. If I lost the job only to discover that Richard was safe and well with Emily, then how would I feed us?

It was the longest week of my life. I'll never know how I found the strength or the will to face that job every day but knowing that I needed this work to provide for Richard helped me to see it through. At last it was my day off and again I took the bus to Davao City to continue my search. *Today will be the day I find my baby*, I convinced myself as the bus pulled into the station. There would be some simple explanation for all of this; I would find Richard and laugh at myself for being so silly. I went straight to Emily's place, certain that she would be there, but the house was vacant and there was not a sign of Richard or her.

My heart sank. It had been more than a week now since Emily and Richard went missing, plenty of time for them to return home if all of this was just something innocent. My stomach felt sick as I faced the fact that, for some reason, Emily had abducted my baby.

Like a mad woman I banged on door after door, begging anyone who would listen for information on Emily and Richard's whereabouts, but nobody had seen sight of them. It was as if a hole in the ground had opened and swallowed them up. I was going crazy. Family or not – despite what my brother had said and my own fears – it was time to go to the police. I could not deal with this on my own any more.

I bought a wig and applied a fake mole to my upper lip with ink and four needles. (I still have the mark to this day, although it is now faded thanks to a tattoo removal procedure I had done in Taiwan.) Thus disguised, I walked nervously into the police station and reported a baby missing. I told them the story exactly as it happened, except I gave false names for me and Richard. But I gave the real name and contact details for Emily. I reasoned that the important thing was to discover where Emily had gone. Wherever she was, Richard would be there also. The police would search for her regardless of the name of the missing baby. If the police found Emily I knew she would be surprised by the name the police were using for Richard and me. I was also sure that she would deny everything and she would certainly not mention my real name or Richard's name to them. Either way, the police would have to report back to me and I would then know where she was. That was all I would need to know.

I had been clinging to the hope that, sooner or later, Emily would have to return to her home, but the police investigation dashed that hope to pieces. Emily did not own the house. She was only a caretaker tenant who had been given free accommodation in the house for so long as she cared for the grounds of a now disused church on which the house sat. I felt the blood rush to my feet and I felt weak as I realised that there was nothing to tie her to this place. I gave the police full information on all of Emily's relatives but I knew this was a waste of time and would not yield any useful information. Davao had gone through a major period of violence and political unrest and, although it was now over the worst of it, there was still suspicion and fear for figures of authority and no one would willingly get mixed up in police business, especially not when it concerned family members.

The police took up and continued the search for Richard and every day I went to Davao City to do my own searching for my baby. I questioned the neighbours again and again, but no matter who I asked, the answer was always the same – no one knew anything. It was exhausting making the eight-hour round journey almost every day, but I had to do it. How else would I find my baby? My supervisor at the Dole plantation was getting increasingly angry at me for taking so much time off work and for my constant nagging at him for leave. He eventually sacked me.

Although I had now officially reported Richard missing and spent months looking for him, to the point of exhaustion, I had to face the fact that, with a population of over seventy-six million in the Philippines, it was like looking for a needle in a haystack.

Hard as I tried, I did not find my baby. I mourned his loss as you would a child who had died, but it was worse than that. There was no closure to this and as much as I tried to forget it and move on, it was always there in the back of my head. It sprung back into life every time I saw a child of Richard's age and with any resemblance to him. I would torture myself wondering if it was him, sometimes following the mother and child to get a better look at the baby. Each time, the disappointment I felt when I discovered it was not him ripped my heart apart and I mourned his loss all over again.

I couldn't understand why my baby had been taken from me. Why my baby? Over and over again I relived the moment when I asked Emily to mind Richard and I agonised, wishing that somehow I could change that moment. If I had not gone into the church that day, the house of God, then none of this would have happened. Had I not already suffered enough? Day after day and week after week, I returned to that church in vain, hoping that I would see Emily again. I asked this terrible God if he hated me so much that he had to give me pain in every part of my life.

I would never give up looking for Richard, my baby, or believing that he was alive out there somewhere, but I had to get a grip back on my life, to find a way to live with this and move on. I had two other children who needed me and I would be of no use to them if I lay down and died. Even though I had not developed any real maternal instincts for Charmie or Charlon, that did not mean I shirked my responsibilities to them. Whether I liked it or not, I was their mother and sooner or later I knew I would have to face that fact and start acting like a mother to them. Although I was sending money to them on a regular basis when I was working in the Dole plantation, with their father still pursuing me there was no way I could even consider having them with me. If they were with me I might as well just put a sign on my head saying, "Here I am – come and get me."

12

Illegitimate Solution

In 1987 news reached me that my husband, who was still looking for me, was getting closer and heading to Polomolok. My stomach felt sick at the thought of him ever coming near me again. I was taking no chances. If he came to Polomolok, then the first place he would come looking for me would be in my brother's apartment or some of my other relatives' houses, so I moved out of that area and into Banaba Street in Polomolok town. Vivian, my friend since childhood and the daughter of Andrea, was working with me in the Dole plantation. Vivian knew all about my past and did not hesitate to move into an apartment with me when she heard that my husband was seeking me out. It was good to have such a friend but I could not keep doing this for the rest of my life – moving like a scared rabbit every time I knew my husband was getting near.

So when Hermie Morales called on me once again, as he had been doing for the past two years, I made a decision. If my husband heard that I was with someone else, then maybe his pride would prevent him from wanting me back and he would leave me alone. This would provide me with the safety I needed and so I decided to accept Hermie Morales into my life.

I did not love him and was not attracted to him physically but he seemed to be a decent man and I thought that over time I would learn to love him. In some ways, it seemed a cold decision to make, but I would have done anything, including killing myself, if it was the only way to ensure that my husband could not get his hands on me again. I needed the protection and security that only a man could give me. I reasoned that we would both be getting something out of it.

He brought me to visit in his parents' house and everything was going along smoothly until he mentioned that I was already married. The atmosphere changed almost instantly and they let me know what they thought of me. If you were a woman in the Philippines and had been in a previous marriage or you were not a virgin getting married, then in the eyes of the man's family, you were less than dirt. An argument took place between Hermie and his parents. We ended up leaving and going back to my apartment. It was the first night we spent together.

Because of the problems with his parents, he moved in with me and we spent a month in the apartment. By the end of that month his parents were horrified that their son was living in town with a married woman, so they told him it would be much better if we moved in with them; it would give the relationship a little more respectability. I was not too keen on the idea and I should have seen the warning signs when he was so quick to march to their tune. However, I did not want to cause problems between him and his family and so I agreed to move in with them.

One thing that really did disturb me was when he told me to tell his parents that I had only two children and not three. He said that if they knew I had a young baby, even if he was missing, they would never accept the two of us. It hurt me to deny Richard, but I reasoned that he was no longer with me anyway, so if this denial was what was required to secure the relationship, I would do it – anything to keep my husband away from me.

We moved in and then the trouble really began. His sister thought that I was not good enough for her brother; she would spit at me whenever she got the chance. It would have been so easy to break her mouth and make her pay for doing that to me, but I had left violence behind me and I was not going to bring it into this house. Instead, controlling my temper, I told her, "Don't do that to me! Who do you think you are? At home, the piggery in my mom's house is better than this. Who are you to spit at me?"

But if it was not his sister then it was his mother gossiping in the street about me and the heads turning every time I walked outside. I could not understand why he was letting his family treat me this way. When I asked him, he said that he had to respect his parents and his family. So I knew where I came in the pecking order. But there was nothing I could do; I had to make this relationship work. It was hard enough being a woman in the Philippines having had one failed relationship behind you, but to have two would be unbearable. As it was, I was considered by his family as the "leavings of someone else".

My kids, Charmie and Charlon, were still with my mom. I wanted to take them now that I had the protection of another man but, with the problems being caused by Hermie's family, I did not want to remove them from an environment in which they were comfortable to one of uncertainty. Hermie had also told me that he was not going to help me look for Richard. "What will we tell my parents if we find him and bring him into the house?" he asked. It was now obvious that he was not going to accept another man's baby. He had told me that he would but now that he had got what he wanted, he changed his tune. It was okay for him to sleep with me but not to accept my flesh and blood. It was doubtful if I would ever see Richard again but I would always think of him as alive and never give up the hope that one day I might find him.

I had also discovered that Hermie was very tight with his money. What was his remained his; he did not share. Without a job, I did not want my kids coming here to this house only to be treated as disrespectfully as I was being treated. Every morsel of food they would eat would be counted and weighed against them.

But at least one thing had worked out for me: on hearing that I was with someone else, my husband stopped looking for me and I later learned that he was with someone else. When I heard the news I said two prayers, one of thanks for my release and one of pity for the other woman. But it saddened me to learn that, since I left, he had not supported his children; he had not spent even one single peso on them.

At every possible opportunity Hermie's family tried to do everything they could to come between us. With the harassment and their taunting of me now an almost daily occurrence, living in that house became unbearable for me. It looked like I was there for their amusement; I was something to poke fun at and to belittle. They were trying to grind me down, to break me and free their son and brother from a woman who, in their eyes was filth. I began feeling nervous, going off my food and suffering from blinding headaches.

I needed a break, even it was only for a couple of hours. I needed to get out of that house and away from that family. My brother Alker and his wife Adela were still living in Cannery so I decided to pay them a visit; it would be good to see them again and an opportunity to relax for a little while. When I returned from my visit, just as I was about to enter the house, I noticed Hermie's ex-girlfriend sitting in a restaurant beside the house. "What is she doing there?" I wondered, immediately smelling a rat. Hermie was working nights so while I was visiting my brother, he was supposedly sleeping before his shift. When I got to our room, I asked him if he was aware that his ex-girlfriend was outside. He tried to explain it away by saying that he had been asleep and that when he awoke she was in his room. When I asked how she had got in, he said that his father had let her in to tempt him and cause trouble between us. I was not buying into that story and a huge row broke out between us.

I wanted to go, to walk away and leave him and his horrible family behind, but I was already two months pregnant with his baby and it was not an option. Stupidly I was also determined not to let his family get their way and split us up. Being pregnant did have one advantage, however; I told him that if I stayed in that house and continued to endure this treatment at his hands and the hands of his family then maybe the baby I gave birth to would be a sick baby.

What I said obviously frightened him because the next week, much to my joy, we moved out of his parents' house and into an apartment owned by my uncle Charlie. I was much happier there and on 31 March 1988 I gave birth to my fourth child, a baby girl. I named her Herlene Rose. She was one month premature and, like her sister and two brothers, she weighed in at exactly four pounds.

The time spent living in Hermie's parents' house and the incident with his ex-girlfriend had taken their toll on me. It had allowed uncertainty to enter our lives and that uncertainty shattered not just my confidence in myself but also my confidence in the relationship. I was twenty-three years old. I would have struggled to count off on the fingers of one hand the number of happy times I had experienced in my life since the time I was raped at sixteen years of age to the time of Herlene's birth.

I had given birth to four children but had never known love. Three of my children had been conceived in violence and, although Hermie was not violent towards me, there was no passion in our relationship. Sex was something that he did for *his* pleasure and when he had taken his pleasure he rolled over and went to sleep. It was cold and, as had been the case in my marriage, albeit for very different reasons, I once again found myself feeling like an object, something that was being *used*. But unlike my forced marriage, I had entered willingly into this relationship for my own purposes and I would not run away from my responsibilities to try and make it work. All of this stuff that was going on inside my brain became too much for my young head to handle and the headaches I had first experienced in his parents' house now increased in their frequency and ferocity.

None of this was helped by Hermie's meanness. His money stayed with him and, after what had happened with his ex-girlfriend, I was not prepared to become dependent on him or be at his mercy for the things I needed in my life. I needed to work, not just for the money but also for my sanity. I wrote a letter to my mom explaining my need to work and she sent me one of her helpers, which freed me from being tied to the house.

I was quick to get a job as a sales clerk in the wholesale department of Kimball Plaza, a shopping mall in General Santos City. General Santos is a good distance from Polomolok and it did not make sense to travel back and forth. I was earning good money and Hermie had sourced a job as a driver for a beer company, so we rented an apartment and made General Santos our new home. There was also the added bonus that being in General Santos City put some much-needed distance between us and his family.

Hermie worked away from Monday to Friday doing deliveries, only coming home at the weekends, so at night I joined karate classes and improved on my self-defence. Things were looking brighter. Although I still did not love the man, I was always accommodating, respectful and loyal to him. I had resigned myself to this life and, while I wanted respect, if love did not have a part to play, then so be it. There were worse things, as I knew only too well.

The break from his parents never happened. They saw our new apartment in General Santos as a holiday home and they spent nearly all of their time there with us. It was not ideal but the fact that I was out working meant that I did not have to be with them all the time, so for the sake of peace I grinned and bore it.

His parents, however, were to be the least of my worries.

One weekend Hermie arrived back at the apartment with two of his workmates. I left them to chat while I went to the kitchen and made something for them to eat. There was laughing and joking but in the midst of all the laughter I heard the word "disco" and then someone saying, "Be quiet, she will hear." Although I was in the kitchen and pretended I had heard nothing I listened intently as the night wore on and tongues became a little looser. By the time the night was over, I had pieced all the snippets of information together. It appeared that Hermie was in a disco in the company of a woman. I was hurt and upset to think that he might have been out partying with another woman behind my back but I didn't let him know what I had heard. Maybe it was not as his workmates had said and I did not want to accuse him in the wrong. I wanted to trust him and did not want to believe he would deliberately hurt me like that. So I sent whatever doubts I had to the back of my mind and put it down to nothing more than some high spirits while on a night out with his friends.

It was not very long after this and while I was working sorting some stock at my counter that I noticed two women close by who were having a chat. I couldn't help but notice that they kept looking in my direction and it soon became clear that they were talking about me. I couldn't hear all of their conversation, but I did hear one of them say, "Yes, I'm sure that's her, she's definitely the wife of Hermie Morales." I wondered why I was the topic of their conversation but as an employee it was not my place to interrupt or interfere in any of the customers' affairs. I could be accused of eavesdropping on their private conversation and I would lose my job. It was probably just some idle gossip which would not have been unusual especially when you were a new arrival.

Of course, although Hermie and I were living together, we were not married at that stage. This was not unusual in the Philippines. With no divorce, the only option for couples where one or both of the parties in the relationship had previously been married was to live together in what the Catholic Church called *sin*. The Catholic Church was very powerful in the Philippines and still is. There is no real separation between Church and State. What the Church said carried weight, and if you were living outside their rules, it could make life very difficult. Having children born out of wedlock was certainly against their rules and we were soon to discover the consequences not just for us but also for our child.

The Social Security Service (SSS) is a government fund provided to support the families of workers in the event of disability or death. It is funded by a contribution deducted from the worker's salary and a contribution for each worker by the employer. A requirement for processing your papers for becoming part of the scheme is for every employee to name their beneficiaries in the event of the government having to make a payout under the scheme. This posed major problems for us. The first was that I was legally married to someone else and not Hermie. In Philippines law, my husband the rapist would be entitled to inherit on my death. The second problem was that, with no divorce in the Philippines I could not remedy this situation. Finally there was the fact that, without Hermie and I being married, our daughter Herlene's status was considered illegitimate and she would not be recognised by the SSS. In fact, because of the Church's influence, Herlene would encounter a lot of difficulties if her status remained illegitimate.

Hermie came up with a solution. "Let's just get married anyway. I can fake your papers, give you a new address, making it look as though you've been living all your life in Tibuli, South Cotabato – with Tibuli being so remote, no one will ever suspect a thing if they search the records," he said, confident in his ability to pull this off.

I was shocked by his suggestion. "But that would be bigamy!"

"Yes, it would be bigamy – but isn't it better to live with that than living with our daughter always being called illegitimate and having no legal status?" he answered forcefully – forgetting to mention that I would be the bigamist, not him. I would be the one breaking the law, not him.

Herlene, of course, was my main concern. I did not want her having the tag "illegitimate" around her neck for the rest of her life and so I agreed to Hermie's plan. He was good to his word and within a few weeks, the fake papers had been accepted and we had approval for the wedding.

The tradition in the Philippines is that the parents of the groom pay for the wedding expenses but because I had been married before, his family would not contribute even one single peso. I wrote to my mom and she shouldered all of the expenses. Even on the day of the wedding his parents still refused to accept me, even though I was showing my commitment to their son and our relationship, not only by getting married to him but by the huge risk I was taking in committing bigamy, a crime that carried a jail sentence. I had given them a granddaughter and overlooked the way I had been cruelly treated by them, yet they continued to treat me as if I was nothing more than an inconvenience.

13

Betrayal

A little over a year later, I was pregnant again with my fifth child. This pregnancy seemed to take a lot out of me physically and my headaches were getting worse. I had never discussed with anyone the problems I had with his family, or the incident with his ex-girlfriend, or even the rumours about him seeing the woman in the disco. I hated gossip and did not want to feed an always hungry audience with details of my life. But I believe that repressing all of these troubles within me was causing the blinding headaches.

One day, I blacked out at work and had to be rushed to hospital by ambulance. The doctors said the blackout was caused by stress and fatigue and that I was mentally and physically exhausted. I was discharged and told to rest and take things easy; but that was more easily said than done. If I did not work then I had no money and, with no money, how was I supposed to survive?

There was a fiesta being held in Champaca Street and I decided to go there, hoping that the celebrations and the fun of the occasion might lift my spirits. As I made my way to the fiesta, I passed a coconut tree and noticed that there was a bull tied to it by a long length of rope. At first it seemed to take little notice of me but as I continued on my way it locked its sights onto me and headed in my direction. I tried not to panic but the rope was so long that it gave the bull all the freedom it needed to reach me if it wanted to. I started to walk more quickly, increasing my pace until it was a slow run but as I did a sudden and unexpected flow of water ran down my legs and I realised in horror that my waters were leaking. I could not stop; I was still within the range of the tethered bull and needed to get a safe distance from it. Thankfully I managed to put enough distance between it and me before it reached the limit of the rope.

I was only six months into my pregnancy and with my waters leaking I worried for my baby. The doctor admitted me to the hospital for two days and put me on medication to enable me to hold onto the baby. I sent word to Hermie, thinking that he would be anxious to see me and speak to the doctors about the health of his unborn child; but he never even bothered to come home or to visit me in the hospital.

When I was discharged I went back to work and my life, trying to ignore what was happening while pretending to everyone that I was okay and that my life was wonderful.

The lady had been hovering around for some time before she finally approached me at the counter and asked, "Are you Luz?" She looked very uneasy.

Wondering how she knew me, I replied, "Yes, why do you ask?"

She fidgeted for a bit and then said, "I am the wife of one of your husband's co-workers and I often stay with them in the warehouse."

Her answer surprised me. "You stay with them? I never knew that wives could stay in the warehouse with their husbands." I did not like the sound of this.

She looked at me and hesitated for a moment before continuing, "Luz, if it's good enough for the mistress to stay there, it's certainly good enough for the wife."

I couldn't speak; I didn't know what to say.

Seeing that I was disturbed by what she was saying, she went on, "Look, Luz, I didn't come here to upset you, but you really need to get yourself over to that warehouse so that you know what's going on there." And with that she said goodbye and left.

I tried to make sense of what she had just told me. The more I churned it around in my head, the more upset I became. Hermie worked away from home five days out of seven. It was a long time for a couple to be apart and yet never once did he mention to me that I could have visited him at the warehouse. Why? Then there had been the rumours about the woman in the disco – had they been true? And why had he not bothered to come home when I was admitted to hospital?

I could feel the tears welling up at the back of my eyes and the dryness in my throat as I tried to swallow but I did not cry and I did not choke on the hurt I had to digest. I would keep these thoughts to myself and concentrate on keeping myself well for the sake of my unborn baby, whose birth was imminent. I was also hanging on to the slender hope that maybe all of these doubts in my head would be shown up as just that – unfounded doubts with no truth attached to them.

On 4 August 1991 I gave birth to my fifth child, a boy, and I named him Hermson Jee. Word was sent to Hermie that I was in labour but he never came to the hospital, only showing up the following morning when I was going home. I never let the anger or the upset show on my face. I simply went home and made out like everything was perfectly normal; but another doubt had been added to the others I had been collecting and stashed to the back of my mind. Now, as I recovered from the birth and cared for my baby, I began to formulate a plan to find the truth.

One month after the birth I returned to work and gave Hermie the illusion that I was the naïve little wife he had always taken me to be. I let him settle back into his routine just long enough for the usual complacency to creep back in. Then I put my plan into action. He must have felt very safe knowing that I finished work at eight o'clock; by that time it was too late to get a bus to his place of work. I wanted to use this to my advantage. So one day after work, instead of going home, I hitched a lift in a fish truck, arriving unannounced at his place of work, the warehouse. The grounds on which the warehouse was situated were accessed through a small door cut into a wall, approximately twenty-five feet high and guarded by armed security. The warehouse was the size of an aircraft hangar and had a separate area at its side which provided sleeping quarters for the staff.

It was eleven o'clock by the time I got there and everyone was surprised when, after clearing security, I walked onto the grounds. One of Hermie's co-workers, who knew me and who had seen me enter the grounds, started to shout in a loud voice, "Hermie, your wife is here!" Obviously, this was not to inform him – it sounded more like he was giving him a warning. I saw the man run and so I gave chase, catching up on him just as he was knocking on the door of a room and repeating his warning, "Hermie, quick, your wife is here." His co-worker did not see me standing behind him and was unprepared when I rushed past him and pushed the door into the sleeping quarters open.

What I saw disgusted me. Hermie, the man I had trusted, the man whose son I had given birth to only weeks before, was having sex with another woman. I had seen that woman's face before – I remembered that she had been one of the two women I had observed talking about me in the store where I worked. She was the one who had said, "That's the wife of Hermie Morales." She must have been laughing behind my back all of this time.

I watched them as an uncontrollable anger welled up inside of me. For the very first time in my life I lost control and became wild as I went for the two of them. Two of the workers held me back and the woman just ran away as quickly as she could. I wanted to get out of there as fast as I could and away from the vile stench of treachery that assaulted my senses. It was too late to get transport back home so I waited for morning to come around. Shaking from the rage that was within me, I told Hermie's co-workers to keep him out of my sight.

At five o'clock the following morning, I got the bus home. I waited for him but he did not come home that night. His parents were staying in my apartment and when I told them what had happened, they would not believe me. Two days later he came into the apartment and I said, "I'm not talking to you here – let's go to the plaza where there are people around, because I have nothing to say to you except that we are finished."

At the plaza I demanded to know, "How could you do this to me? I have done everything you ever asked of me – put up with abuse from your family, given birth to your children – and still you can do this to me! Why?"

"One of my friends set it up for me," he replied, as if that made it okay. He was expecting me to accept that this woman was a gift he just couldn't refuse.

"Oh I understand, now," I replied, taunting him. "So if you come home from work some day and I'm having sex with some other guy, I'll say it's just because my friend set it up for me and will you leave us alone for an hour or two – and that will be okay for you, will it?"

He sat there contemplating the stupidity and insulting nature of the reason he had given me. Of course, there was no answer to justify what he had done. He was still lying to me because I knew he had been seeing this woman regularly. It was not something his friends had set up. His excuse was a familiar one – it echoed the incident with his ex-girlfriend, when he had told me it was his father who sent her into his room. I remembered the way his whole family had treated me as if I was dirt.

I took my jacket and stood up from the table.

"Where are you going?" he asked.

"To your parents, Hermie, that's where I'm going. Aren't you coming too?" I asked, walking away.

When I got to the apartment his father was already standing in the door, ready to greet me with his fists, waving them in my face and calling me a liar for what I was saying about his son.

"How can you call me a liar? Did *you* see what I saw with my own two eyes?" I shouted back at him.

It was a big mistake for him to make a fist at me. When I was a young frightened girl, I had accepted fists being pounded into my body, but never again. Putting my face right up to his, I said, "Go on, try me! Do it and see what happens!" Looking him squarely in the eyes, I continued, "Don't mistake my quietness and acceptance of all the abuse you and your family have thrown at me as weakness. I accepted all of that out of respect to your son, but I no longer owe him any respect. So be very, very careful. And if by some miracle you had managed to hit me or mark me, then what do you think my family, my godfather and my cousin would do if I showed them." I shouted, challenging him to go as far as he dared.

No one had ever seen this side of me and I knew they were shocked by my words and actions. I could forgive a lot and try to understand anyone's point of view, but even if it meant I had to die defending myself, no one would ever lay a hand on me again.

We went into the apartment and he pleaded with me not to leave. He promised to leave his job and find work elsewhere, anything I wanted, so long as I did not leave. I looked at the kids and saw in their little faces the real victims of his treachery and my revenge if I were to leave him. There was also the unfair reality that in the Philippines there were different sets of standards for men and women. A man could have his mistresses and as many affairs as he could manage and no one would chastise him. In fact, in some cases, it was something they would boast about. The woman was supposed to accept her husband literally "for better or for worse" and adopt the role of martyr, accepting all his wrongdoings, and at all costs preserving the marriage.

Even in my situation, when my workmates later heard what had happened, their reaction was not to say, "Oh my God, you need to get rid of him," or, "That's terrible, how could he do that to you? Don't ever trust him again." Instead they took me aside and applied make-up to my face, teaching me how to make myself more attractive for my husband, even describing sexual techniques that I should master to keep him satisfied in bed. The purpose of all this was to keep his attention on me and not on his mistress. In other words, I was to turn myself into a slut and compete with the tart he was screwing.

If, on the other hand, a woman was to have an affair or be caught cheating on her husband, well, she had better find some hole in the ground to hide in, because her life would not be worth living, such would be the outcry over her actions. Even the law was stacked in favour of the man if the marriage broke down. It is fair to say that marriage in the Philippines for a lot of women is not just a sacrament that you dare not break on peril of losing your soul but also a life sentence to be served behind bars of hypocrisy and without any hope of reprieve.

"Okay then, do it – don't talk about it, change your job and prove to me that I can trust you and believe in your words," I said, having weighed up the consequences for me and the children if I walked out now.

He changed his job and promised me he would never let me down again, but despite his words and his actions I just could not bring myself to trust him or believe him. I tried to act as if everything was normal and from the outside it looked like we had patched up our problems, but inside the apartment the atmosphere was changed and we rowed constantly. The pains in my head got so bad now that the hospital was becoming like a holiday home for me, so frequent were my visits for treatment. The torment of wondering where he was and what was he doing every time he left the house without me was exacerbating the problem.

That is what happens once the trust is gone. No matter how well you repair the cracks, you're still left dealing with something that was broken and you are now only too aware of how easily it can be broken again. It was no use. I had tried but it was not working and I did not want to go on living a tortured life. I had not survived physical torture in my first marriage only to succumb to the mental torture being dished out to me in this one.

Ardina, one of my workmates, had a visitor in her home, a woman called Mrs Quesumbing, who owned a recruitment agency. She asked me if I would like to meet her. Ardina, along with another of my workmates Editha, would soon be flying to Manila on their way to work in Mrs Quesumbing's recruitment agency in Taiwan. I was introduced to Mrs Quesumbing and she told me that I was very welcome to stay in her house in Manila should

I decide to go there with Ardina and Editha. It was the chance I had been hoping for and the answer to my prayers. I could get away from everything and make a fresh start.

It was the ambition of everyone who lived in the provinces to get to Manila someday. In our eyes it was sophisticated and offered a real chance to escape the dreariness of our ordinary lives. I think it compares favourably to how people in Ireland once imagined that the streets of London were paved with gold. The grass always appears greener on the other side of the fence but for me I didn't care if there was no grass there at all when I arrived. I just wanted the chance to grow my own.

I told Hermie that I could not continue living with him and what he had done, pretending that things were back to normal when they were not and never would be. Our relationship had been destroyed by lies and deceit. We agreed for the sake of the children and as a ploy to prevent malicious chat and gossip that we would just tell everyone that I had gone to Manila to seek work. Because of the uncertainty of my situation I suggested that the children stay with him and his family. It would be hard enough to find my own feet in a sprawling city like Manila without having the added burden of the children to think about.

All around me I could observe women who, broken and abused, were old before they ever had a chance to be young. Manipulated and controlled by their cheating and abusive husbands, they were victims of an ingrained and misplaced sense of duty to which they were conditioned and brainwashed from the day they were born. Marriage for most women in the Philippines was the surrendering of who you were, consigning yourself as a possession of your husband, elevating him to the status of your master and subject to his every whim. But not me, not any more. I'd had enough of men and their cruel ways. I had cared for his children from the moment they were born, been a good mother and a devoted wife, but he had destroyed that. Now he and his family could play the role of devoted parent and grandparents. I was going in search of a life.

14

Home Truths

Manila is a two-hour flight from General Santos. As well as being the capital of the Philippines, it is one of the seventeen cities and municipalities that make up the greater metropolitan area of Metro Manila. It is located on the shores of Manila Bay, west of the geographical centre of Metro Manila. The city has a population of approximately 1.6 million, with the greater metropolitan area being home to some fourteen million people. Life in the provinces is simple and goes on at a relaxed and sometimes lazy place; Manila, however, was something completely different. With its imposing skyscrapers and the seemingly never-ending movement of people all scurrying through its often-blocked arteries, I found it a scary place to be. In the provinces you would know almost everyone in your area, but here there were so many people all occupying and living in this bustling city that it left me feeling vulnerable, lost and alone.

Thankfully I had Editha and Ardina for company, and the three of us had Mrs Quesumbing as our host and guide. Mrs Quesumbing gave me a job in her recruitment agency and I was delighted to be working and busy again. I was responsible for processing the papers, visas and plane tickets of all the applicants applying to work abroad, which involved me dealing with the various embassies, the department of foreign affairs and so on. I really liked the work and the experience it was providing me with.

In the evenings or whenever I had some free time, I went to my uncle's shipping company at the docks and learned all about the business of being a cargo agent. (Strictly speaking, he was a cousin of my mother and not my uncle but in the Philippines we had been brought up to call these members of our family *uncle*.) Eventually my uncle gave me some part-time work checking goods on and off the international cargo ships. It felt good to be learning all of these new skills, challenging myself and improving my life.

Some of Mrs Quesumbing's family, including her daughter and her daughter's baby, were staying over in the house with Editha, Ardina and me while Mrs Quesumbing was out on some business. One day, a policeman from Makati, Manila, called to the house. He was looking for Mrs Quesumbing and explained to us that he had paid her 80,000 peso – a lot of money – as a placement fee for finding work for his wife abroad. It was now months since he had handed the money over but his wife had not received any news of the job. He was furious and explained how he had borrowed the money for the placement in the belief that he would be able to pay it back through his wife's new job. I understood his anger and knew he would really explode if I told him that his wife's papers had been denied and that there was no job. I had no idea that he had not been refunded. I was only an employee and knew nothing of the internal dealings of the company. This was not my problem and I was certainly not going to tell him what I knew while he was in this state of anger.

"As you can see, Mrs Quesumbing is not here, but I will talk to her when she comes home and tell her that you were here," I said.

He accepted this but before he left he said, "Tell her to make sure she is here tomorrow; otherwise, I will find her and kill her." I could tell by his eyes that he meant it.

When Mrs Quesumbing arrived home I told her what had happened. She seemed shaken but, saying nothing, she turned on her heels and left the house immediately. Three hours later she rang to say she had fled and was hiding out in a hotel, but not before she had gone to the military barracks and reported the threat on her life. She told us that ten airborne military paratroopers were being sent to the house to protect us.

I couldn't believe what I was hearing. Even here in the city, away from the remote and often lawless places I had left behind, trouble and the threat of violence had still managed to find me. I called my cousin Crispin and asked him to come to the house, as I no longer felt safe there. It was scary being in the house that night. For military troops to be deployed, as they had been at Mrs Quesumbing's request, was highly unusual. She had obviously exercised some influence to make it happen, but we never discovered what it was. We learned from neighbours that the Makati policeman had been informed about the troops and he was obviously fearful of returning to the house, as he promised that he would, without the backup of the Makati police force. The airborne soldiers were outnumbered and trapped inside the house with the rest of us. What would happen next was anyone's guess. All it needed was one itchy trigger and I could find myself in the middle of crossfire.

A loud bang on the door made us jump. We heard the voice of the police officer who had been in the house the previous day ordering us to open up. It was best if a civilian answered him. I opened the door and said, "Listen to me, I did as you asked and told her you were looking for her – but she has gone into hiding and we don't know where she is." He didn't respond, so I continued, "We're only civilians; there is a baby in here with us and the airborne are only here to protect us. We are innocent in all of this we don't know what your business is with her."

Thank God he was satisfied with my explanation and I could take my hand away from the knife I had tucked into the back of my jeans. With the crisis over, we all breathed a sigh of relief.

After this experience, it was time to resign from that job and get out of that house, or maybe one day I would be the wrong person in the wrong place at the wrong time.

It was 1995. My auntie worked in the Philippines Port Authority; on her advice, I applied for a job with Singa

Ship Management Phils Inc, where they gave me an interview and I sat their exam. I was delighted when I came in the top three of all the people interviewed and tested. It meant that I would receive free training as a sea woman from the Cunard Line.

Of course, I considered what this would mean for the kids and to my mind it was all positive. Charmie and Charlon were in Lambajon with my mother and Herlene and Hermson were in Polomolok with Hermie's family. Both Lambajon and Polomolok were a long way from Manila and for all that it mattered I might as well be living in another country, so great was this distance. Working on the ship would not in reality make me feel any farther away from them than I already was. But working on the ship *would* give me an opportunity to earn the money that would give me my independence. If I worked really hard, I could build a home and take my kids to live with me. We would be a family and I would do my best to be a good mother.

Whenever I thought of or mentioned us as a family, I always included Richard. By this time, it was nine years since my son had been abducted. I often wondered how he would look now. Would I even know him if he were to stand right in front of me? It was a thought I did not like to entertain. To think that my son could pass by me unnoticed was just too upsetting. When I was in Polomolok and General Santos, I had continued my search for Richard whenever possible and then when I moved to Manila I had arranged for my family to continue the search. The searches always came to nothing and it took a lot of strength not to give in to the feelings of hopelessness. Pulling myself together, I would say, "Next time, maybe next time, Richard."

My first ship was the *Royal Viking Sun* and I boarded her in Hong Kong as a florist responsible for providing the floral displays throughout the ship. One day, I brought a fresh arrangement to a passenger's cabin at his request. "Will you put them on the table over there?" he said, pointing to the table in his cabin. I obliged, but as soon as I was at the table, I heard the cabin door being locked behind me. "Whatever you are thinking of doing, don't," I warned as I backed away from him. "It's okay, I won't tell anyone or report you, so you won't lose your job," he answered me back, as if he was somehow going to be doing me a favour by forcing sex on me. "You may not be going to report it, but I certainly will, the moment I get out of this room," I said, moving to one side of the bed. He made a lunge at me and missed, falling off balance. I seized the opportunity to jump across the bed, unlocked the door and escaped.

I did report him to the captain, threatening that if he did not take action against the passenger I would file a case. The captain was horrified and when we docked in the USA he threw the passenger off and then ensured that he was banned from all other cruise ships. Obviously, I would have preferred if this entire incident had never happened, but I had proven to myself that even on my own and outside the familiarity of my own country for the first time in my life, I really did have the strength to stand up for myself. I had come a long way.

It was an upsetting incident but it proved to be the only bad time in a job and time in my life that I really loved. I could not believe that, whenever the ship docked in a different part of the world, I was actually setting foot in places I had only ever seen in magazines or on TV – the Pyramids, the Sydney Opera House, the Eiffel Tower, the Holy Land, Russia, the Caribbean, Asia, Europe, the USA, Alaska, the North and South Poles, and other wonderful and exotic places . . . I was seeing them all. It was a wonderful and exciting time. I used to write home to my mom and my family and tease them by saying, "Imagine – I just dust and clean a little and in return I get to see the world."

I soon transferred from being the florist to being an entertainment stewardess and also took a food and hygiene course. It was great to see the world and I was also now making serious money. As a penthouse stewardess, my salary was $500 per month, but the wages were nothing compared to my tips which, at their very lowest, were amounting to $3,500 per month. I was working really hard, never refusing any extra work that came my way, but it would all be worth it because I was earning and saving this money for my future and it was honest money earned from my own sweat.

While the ship was docked in Yalta, Ukraine, in 1996, I received a letter from Hermie saying that he was sorry and that he wanted us to get back together again. We had split in 1993. It's said that absence makes the heart grow fonder and maybe that was why, against all my better instincts, I considered his proposal. I missed the kids and although I was sending money back to them on a regular basis, I wanted to be part of a real family. So I accepted him back and arranged for my salary to be sent to him and also extra cash.

This money was to be used to build our own house and an apartment block consisting of four apartments. I also sent the money to buy three "tricycles" – motorbikes with side cars attached for transporting paying passengers. The house would be our home and the apartments and the tricycles would provide a steady income. I also told him that as soon as the house was completed, I wanted to take the children from my mother and bring them to live with us in that house. It was my house, built from my sweat, and nobody was going to tell me who could or could not live in it with me. I was financially independent now and could provide for my children's needs without asking anyone for anything.

I would be finishing my current tour of duty on the ship in December 1997 and Hermie said that he would arrange a church wedding to renew our vows and to show his commitment by having the relationship blessed. While the house and the apartment were being built, they sent pictures of the construction to me. I had mixed feelings when I saw them. I had given Hermie clear plans and designs for how I wanted the house to be built and styled and, while I was happy to see my very own home being constructed at last, I was sad to see he had not followed my plans. It was the same with the apartment block. When I asked why, I discovered that his father was taking charge of the building. It angered me so much. Once again, even though it was my money, there was still this total disrespect for women and unshakable belief that they knew better than me. But I was not going to let it get in the way of my plans to be part of a happy family together again with all of my children under the one roof.

When I got back home things seemed to have improved for the better and I was happy that, at last, life here would be different. I had my new home to look forward to and all of my family were there to greet me for the wedding. There was a marquee erected in front of the house, as the wedding and blessing was taking place that very same day.

When the wedding ceremony and the blessing were over, I started to have a proper look around. I noticed that there was another new house beside my house and, wondering who my neighbour was, I asked Hermie, "Who owns that house?"

"Oh that's my brother's house," he said, standing back and admiring it.

"That's great, I'm really happy for them that they're doing so well."

Our chat was interrupted when his mother called him away, but it gave me an opportunity to go into our house and check out the new cabinets I had bought for the bedroom. When I opened the drawers I was surprised to find receipts from hotels in Davao, General Santos and Marbel. He couldn't afford a lifestyle that included the extravagances of hotels. There was only one explanation for all of this and it made me want to throw up.

"What are these?" I demanded, throwing the receipts at him when he entered the bedroom.

At first he tried to say they were from someone he was driving around who was regularly meeting a woman in hotels, but I was not buying that. Eventually he admitted he had used the hotels himself for women and even picked up a prostitute on one of these occasions.

Adding insult to injury, he told me, "I can't have sex with you. I'm afraid I might have picked something up from the prostitute and I could pass it on to you. You might then fail your medical for your return to work on the ship."

"Do you think I would let you near me after what you have done to me? Do you?" I shouted back at him in disgust. Even after his treachery had been revealed, all he could think of was that he didn't want to be the cause of his money-making wife not being able to earn and send money back to him!

He disgusted me. How could he stand in a church, talk about blessings and speak of commitment, when all the time he had been screwing around behind my back? I had been working every hour that I possibly could to earn money for us, often falling asleep on my bed from exhaustion before I even got a chance to change out of my working clothes. All this time he been spending *my money* earned with *my sweat* to pay for his women and his hotels!

Then, when I thought it couldn't get any worse, my attention once again switched to the new house that his brother had built. Something wasn't right. "Where exactly did your brother get the money to build that house?" I asked suspiciously, hoping against hope that I wasn't going to hear what I thought I was going to hear.

"I gave him some of our money." The words were like daggers in my heart.

"*Our* money – what do you mean *our* money? Did you earn it? Did you?" I screamed the question at him. My fist went through the glass table-top in a fit of temper.

How had I been so stupid? How had I let him do this to me? I realised now that it was not the absence that had made his heart grow fonder, it was the money that I was earning. I told him to get out.

Alone once again with only my regrets and tears for company, I waited for the morning to come around. I flew back to Manila, reported back to the agency, took my medical and went back to the ship.

News reached me that one of the women where he was working was his girlfriend. I remembered how I had entertained him and her, serving them snacks in the apartment after he had introduced her to me as a workmate – and all the time he was having sex with her behind my back. Was there no low to which he would not stoop to humiliate me?

I threw myself back into my work, trying to forget the fool that I had been. I worked in lots of different areas in the ship now – the bar, the officers' mess, the crew mess and so on – and in the year 2000 I was selected to be photographed for the Cunard brochure.

When my tour of duty ended in November 2000 and while I was in Manila, my auntie called me and said that my uncle, who was working in the recruitment agency, was hiring staff for a new Disney Island being built in Hong Kong. She suggested I should apply if I was interested in the work. She also asked me to tell anyone else I knew who might be qualified and interested. I told one person about the work, but I was shocked when lots of people I didn't know started sending their papers to me.

Many Filipino people have ambitions to work and earn money abroad. When it became known that my uncle was working in the hiring agency, others thought that somehow I could help them and so their papers came flooding in. There was very little I could do for them other than to bring their applications to my uncle so that they would be read. I didn't know that this simple act of kindness would be putting me in danger.

One day about one hundred of these applicants arrived in Manila looking for me. Some had no passports, others no medical, and most had nowhere to stay in Manila. Most of them were young people whose parents out of desperation had sent them to Manila with only enough money for transport. I felt sorry for them because I realised that all they wanted was a chance to make a better life for themselves and their families. I spent my own money to help as many of them as I could, in some cases paying for medical expenses, passport applications or even for accommodation.

Manila is not a cheap place to live and very quickly all my money was gone and I was broke. Unfortunately, the hiring was a failure because the company switched to a different recruitment agency. But that was not the end of it. Some of the applicants had spent money going on training courses in order to meet the requirements for the jobs on offer but, with no jobs available through the agency, they had wasted their money.

I could not believe it when they started turning on me. I had nothing to do with the agency and I was not profiting from the applicants going there or working abroad. I had out of kindness presented their papers to

My First Holy Communion, ArdScoil Éanna, Crumlin Road, Dublin.

A family portrait; **back, left to right:** my stepfather, my elder brother Alker and my mother; **front, left to right:** my younger sister Enday, my half-brother Ricky, then me sitting with my half-brother Ronnie on my knee, and finally my brother Alton junior. Only the smiles on the children's faces are missing.

The innocent majorette with some of the band members. Minutes after this photo was taken, my life was brutally changed forever.

Precious moments: me with Richard at three months old – just nine months before he was kidnapped.

Me with my daughter Herlene.

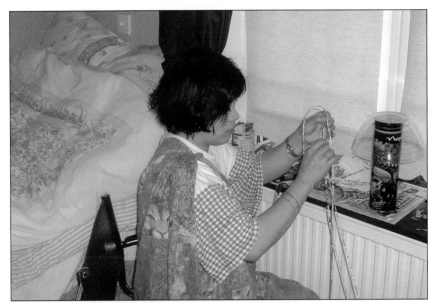

Above: Developing a technique for our invention, using the window sill as a workbench and sitting beside our desk, which also doubled as our bed.

Talking the talk: demonstrating to buyers at the Australian Toy Fair 2006, held at the Olympic Stadium, Sydney.

Tea for two: there is nothing rubbish about these items – the bags, the placemats, the coasters, the flower vase cover, the purse and the picture on the wall are all made from paper waste using the Paper FX Dream Weaver.

We did it: flowers and champagne presented to us after an incredibly successful launch of our products at the 2006 UK Toy Fair.

Holding a dream: the Paper FX Dream Weaver arrives from the manufacturer and finally we put our hands on a dream.

In the house of our good friend Steve Lennon I attempt to build Tumba while Luz looks on and tries to put me off.

One year after the launch, we are presented with a certificate at the 2007 UK Toy Fair, declaring the Paper FX Dream Weaver to be Creative Toy of the Year.

Together again; from left to right: I am so very happy as Charmie hugs me tightly while my niece Adelyn and daughter Herlene complete the happy scene.

Family matters: surrounded by and a part of people who love and care for me, Noel's family.

In Hamleys of London with Noel's sister Lorraine, whose birthday provided the need to invent the card that started the dream.

The dream grows: the Paper FX Dream Weaver, Paper Creation, Tumba – products born of a dream and a lot of love. (Photo © Morgan Studios)

What it is all for: the smiling children of San Juan Village, Agdao, Davao City, Philippines.

Looking to the future, Noel and Luz: inseparable. (Photo © Morgan Studios)

my uncle and left myself broke in the process of trying to help them. Now, just because I was the one who had presented their papers, they tried to blame me.

I could have just walked away and let them stew in their own juices but I am not made like that. I contacted all of the agencies that I knew or had friends in and tried to get them to look after as many of them as possible. Lots of them got work abroad in places like Saudi Arabia, Singapore, Hong Kong, and some in Ireland. Although they were very quick to ask for and accept my help, very few of them were as quick to thank me. I was so broke after helping all of them that I had to pawn my jewellery to pay my living expenses.

I was due to go back to the ship but an opportunity also arose for me to work in Ireland if I wanted it. I already had lots of experience from working on the ship but had never worked on a land base abroad, so I decided I would give Ireland a try.

15

The Prayer

On 20 February 2001, I arrived in Ireland. I was excited to take up my new position as a chambermaid in a hotel in Dublin. But when I got my first pay packet, I was so disappointed; for two weeks' work, I had received just €200. I worked overtime to try to increase my pay, but it was a big mistake. The hotel only paid me their regular rate. Even when they called me to work on my day off and I had been expecting to receive double pay, I still got paid the regular rate. Sometimes they even called me to work evenings in the restaurant and when I obliged they again only paid me the regular hourly rate.

It was exploitation and although I knew it, I also knew that if I complained or rocked the boat, the employer could make life very difficult for me. At that time it was not as easy as it is now for foreign workers to change employers; your contract for work was specifically with your employer and many of them exploited that fact. A lot of foreign workers feared that, if they prematurely lost their job and returned home with no money, they might never find the means to work abroad again. I was thinking of going back to the ship because, even though my work there was very hard, at least I had reward in my pay packet for it.

After I had been in Ireland about three months, I noticed that there was a big market for health foods and food supplements, products I was very familiar with. When I was living in Polomolok, I had spent some time selling health products. I had to, as my husband never gave me any money and it was the only way I could buy the things I needed for me and the kids. My knowledge of these products gave me the confidence to pursue an idea. I sourced products from companies in Malaysia that made health foods derived from a certain type of mushroom and were very successful throughout Asia. I made an arrangement with them that if I could process the papers required to allow the products to be distributed in Ireland, then I would be appointed as the main distributor of the product for Ireland and the UK.

Unfortunately, a huge amount of EU legislation had to be navigated and complied with before I could bring the products into Ireland. It was demoralising at times. First there was the Irish Medical Board, then the Department of Health and Children, and of course the Food Safety Authority. It would have been daunting enough to deal with all of these particular organisations had I been in my own country, but trying to do it in Ireland, through a system I understood very little about was exhausting.

Then, when I went to register the business name, I discovered that as a foreign national I required a

"Business Permission" before I would be permitted to carry out business in Ireland. There are only so many hours in the day, and with this extra condition and the processing it involved, I decided it was time to get help. I contacted a solicitor called Susan Battye and she took my file. Being able to pass this workload over to Susan took a huge weight off my shoulders and I felt that I would now make some real progress.

While I was awaiting the outcome of all of this, I continued to work in the hotel. I tried as best as I could to ignore the low salary and the fact that I was being taken advantage of; but by the year 2002 I'd had enough and handed in my notice to quit. My general manager refused to accept it, telling me he didn't want me to leave and offering me a wage increase. I decided to accept his offer and give it another try.

It had been another hard day's slog. As I turned the key in the lock of my apartment, looking forward to finally being able to put my feet up, I heard the phone ringing and rushed to answer it before it rang out. It was Charmie.

"Hi, Ma! Sorry if I shock you with what I am going to ask – but can I have your consent to marry my boyfriend?"

"*Boyfriend*? Are you pregnant, Charmie?" The question shot out as if by its own command.

"No, Ma, it's not like that. Roly has asked me to marry him and I would like to accept his proposal, with your consent."

Although I had not been home in many years, we still talked on the phone, but Charmie had never mentioned anything about a boyfriend. I questioned her for a long time about Roly and, although I had never met him, I knew of his family. They were a good family but it did not stop the disappointment I was feeling at her wanting to marry so young. She was only twenty years old and I knew only too well how precious those young years are. I had hoped that Charmie would make something more of her life than I had. I had already started the process of getting her work on the ships. It was a great opportunity.

Over the following weeks, I spoke with Roly's parents and voiced my concerns – concerns that they also shared. But none of it mattered. Both Charmie and Roly had their hearts set on marriage and, after offering my advice, all I could now do was respect and support their love and their decision. Mindful of the disappointments in my life, I did however, have some words with Roly before giving my consent.

"Roly, don't hurt my daughter. If for some reason in the future you no longer love her, then give her back to me the way I now give her to you, but *don't hurt her*."

I left no doubt in his mind as to the consequences if he ignored those words. My mam may have sacrificed me to a monster but never, for as long as I had a breath in my body, would I let anyone abuse my daughters.

I was sad that I was unable to attend Charmie's wedding. I didn't have the money to buy a plane ticket, and even if I did, I knew I would not get the time off work and I could not afford to breach the conditions of my work permit. I sent Charmie the money for everything she needed for her wedding. On her wedding day, I lay on my bed, closed my eyes and tried to sleep before the tears and the disappointment of missing another milestone in my daughter's life overcame me.

Unfortunately, as a result of my wage increase, my duties in the hotel were changed. Every morning I worked in the restaurant from seven to nine and then I went straight to work in accommodation until four o'clock in the afternoon. By six o'clock in the evening, I was back in the restaurant and did not finish there until ten o' clock. It was very hard going and it left me very tired, but I have never been afraid of hard work.

One morning I came down to the restaurant early to have some breakfast before I started my shift. Just as I was about to start drinking some orange juice, I was called by two of the supervisors. "Luz, you are not allowed to eat breakfast. Here, use this mop and bucket and clean the stairs." They ordered me as if I was a slave and not a worker.

"How dare you speak to me like that? You deny me a breakfast and yet you don't mind knocking on the door of my room on my time off when you need help! And you don't even pay me the proper rate when I oblige you!" I said furiously, kicking the bucket and throwing the mop under the stairs. I continued, "I'm not stupid – cleaning the stairs is not my job, and someone gets paid overtime for that. I know I am a foreigner here and maybe I don't know what happens next if I have no job but never again will I work for you." With that I walked out.

A few days later, I went back to collect my salary and the plane ticket they owed me as part of my contract for my return flight home. If I could not get another job, I was going to fly home and go back working on the ship. They refused to give me my ticket; no matter how much I argued with them, they would not give it to me. I was leaving the hotel furious over their treatment of me when I met one of the Irish girls who worked there. She advised me to go to the Department of Social Welfare for support while I was looking for another job because, as a taxpayer, I was entitled to it.

After I had received my third social welfare payment, I went to their offices and gave the cheque back to the man on the counter. I told him, "Please take this back, I don't want it. I want a job, I want to work."

He looked at me as if I was mad. "But this is your money! You're entitled to it, you need it."

Yes, I did need it, but to me it felt like I was receiving a handout, so I told him, "Look, I have two hands and two feet. I am not disabled in any way, I want to work for my money, so please keep the cheque and let me know if you have any work."

The look of bewilderment on his face as I walked away is something I will never forget.

I called my daughter Charmie in the Philippines and told her to sell my three tricycles and send the money to me so that I could pay for my flat. Charmie laughed, "Ma, it's usually the other way around, the Filipino working abroad is the one to send the money back home."

But Charmie had something else to tell me and I almost collapsed from shock when she delivered the news. "Ma, you are not going to believe this, but you are going to be so happy! We have found Richard."

I stood with the phone to my ear, refusing to accept what I had just heard.

"Ma, are you there? Did you hear what I just said?"

Finally, I found my voice. "Yes, Charmie, I heard you but I can't take in what you're telling me."

Old, deeply buried emotions stirred within me. I again saw the face of my one-year-old baby, who would now be a seventeen-year-old teenager.

"How, Charmie? How has this happened?" I asked, as the joy of what I was hearing began to take hold and I allowed myself to believe it was true.

"Auntie Fern came across some of Emily's family by accident and through them we traced Richard," Charmie replied excitedly. "When you left Richard with Emily, she took him to Davao Del Sur and that's where he has been living."

No wonder I hadn't been able to find Richard. Davao Del Sur is a nine-hour journey by Jeep from Davao City. Charmie went on to tell me that, even after making that journey, it took a walk of several kilometres through rough mountainous terrain before you could reach the house where Richard had been taken.

"Ma, there is someone here who wants to talk with you."

Suddenly, her voice was replaced by that of a young man.

"Hello, Ma, this is Richard."

I could not believe I was hearing his voice, a voice I thought I would never hear.

"Hello, son." I just about managed to get the words out before I broke down and sobbed with the joy and the pain of all the missed years of my baby's life.

From then on, we spoke to each other whenever we could over the phone.

Charmie explained that Emily had abducted Richard for a family member who had no young children. I wanted to kill her for what she had done, but what good would that do me? It would not bring back the lost years or erase the past. I could have taken legal action against all of them for what they did, but I had to be sensitive to the fact that, whether I liked it or not, those people who Richard had lived with were for all intents and purposes the only family he had known. I was not going to damage him any more than he obviously must have been damaged by the revelations that had been made known to him. Having to challenge everything that he thought he knew about himself could destroy him. I was just happy to have him back in my life and I resolved not to look back at the years that were behind but to look forward to all that lay in front of us.

It was so hard being here in Ireland and knowing that the son I thought I had lost forever was found and still I could not see him. It was also difficult to discuss his life and ask all the questions I had for him because, without seeing him and gauging his reaction, I worried that I would upset him. It would have to wait until somehow I got back to the Philippines.

I was now more determined than ever before to make something out of my life. I received the money that Charmie sent from the sale of my tricycles and it bought me some extra time while I figured my next move. I went to the immigration office in O'Connell Street to see if they could help me in getting the plane ticket I was entitled to from the hotel. I really wanted to return home, both to see Richard and to apply for the ship again; at least there I would earn some decent money. The immigration office appointed a solicitor to the case but she was useless. If I was going to get a plane ticket back home then I was going to have to find work and buy one myself.

I started working in a hotel in Ballyfermot. It was better than the previous hotel but it was still very much a hand-to-mouth existence and offered me no real chance of saving money or building anything for my future. I had visions of myself being an old woman and still making beds and sweeping floors. It was an image I never discarded. Whenever I was feeling down or complacent I would resurrect that image and it spurred me on to do better.

I worked in the hotel for about three months and purely by chance I got an opportunity to work as a masseuse and share in the profits of a new business in the city centre. While completing my secretarial course in Lambajon all those years ago, during the summer break I had enrolled in a course to study reflexology. It had offered yet more distraction from the horror that was my life at that time. I originally applied with a friend of mine to do security in the new business, but when the employer saw on my CV that I was qualified in reflexology and massage, he suggested opening a massage studio. I considered his proposal and put one of my own to him. If I was to open the studio then I would have to be a partner in this business. He agreed and so I began setting up the massage studio.

I was excited by all of this. It was not my own business but because I would be sharing in the profits and I was the one setting it up, it felt like I was in control. At last I would be able to reap the full benefit from my hard work. My future would be in my own hands now and I would make this a success, even if it killed me.

My excitement for the business and my perception of massage were very quickly changed, however. In the Philippines, massage is everywhere – in the shopping centres, at the beaches, even by the side of the road. It's a way of life and everyone can avail of massage, from very young children to very old men and women. That's the way I thought it was going to be here. Yes, in places like Manila, as in all major cities around the world, there were seedy operators with practices that had nothing to with massage. Usually, though, these places were in dedicated areas and everyone knew what they were.

In my innocence, I thought that a main street in Dublin would be free from establishments such as this. I thought that the people frequenting it would be genuine clients looking for massage therapy. But as soon as the phone calls started to come in to make appointments, I knew by the questions I was being asked – such as, "How much do you charge for extras?" – that I had made a big mistake. I was horrified that most of the men calling were only interested in sex and that their perception was that, because I was Asian, I was easy pickings. Now I understood why, when trying to solicit new clients in the area, I would get funny looks from people when I enthusiastically and innocently told them I had opened a massage studio.

I did not want to be associated with this sort of thing and I was really getting irritated by the perverts on the phone. So, after working there for only one month, I resigned my position and left. Susan Battye was still processing the papers for my business permission but it looked like it was going to be some considerable time before she had any worthwhile news for me. I had to pay for my flat and feed myself and so with no other option open to me, I started cleaning houses to earn the money to pay my bills. It was very hard work and the money was not great. The owners of the dirtiest houses seemed to be the ones who wanted to pay me the least amount of money. Then there were the houses where, because they knew you were coming, the owners left the place like a pigsty until you arrived to clean it up.

I really missed home now. If I was going to have to scrimp to survive then it was better I do it in my own country, where at least I would have the pleasure of being with my kids instead of being here and all alone. All my hopes in Ireland were hanging on me securing my business permission and getting the health foods importing up and running.

When I reached this part of my story, I told Noel that this brought me to where I was now in my life and my meeting him that day. I did not tell him that, just the previous night, I had arrived back at my apartment and flopped down onto the bed, exhausted by a gruelling day of cleaning houses and travelling from one end of the city to the other. Alone with my thoughts, I pondered my life and how, despite all of my hard work and good intentions, it had amounted to nothing more than this small rented flat, a few paltry possessions and had become a struggle for survival.

I remembered the bright-eyed innocent sixteen-year-old majorette in her dazzling white uniform, smiling with a head full of dreams and a life full of possibilities, as she rested against the post of the cottage, enjoying the laughter of her friends. I wanted to reach out to her, to feel her again and to tell her to run and never stop running. "Run, Luz, run – and don't ever look back." The words escaped my mouth as a whisper and I tasted my tears as the memories flooded in. I missed her, I missed her dreams and I wanted to be her again. She was the real me and I was only getting to know her, to enjoy being her, when rape stole her away. I couldn't stem the flow of tears as I wondered how her life might have been if she had done something different that day or had simply not been in that place at that time. Would she have met and been romanced by her prince and discovered the joys of life and the wonder of falling in love? Would she have taken to stages all over the world singing her songs, as she dreamed she would every time she brushed her hair and sang into the hairbrush? Would she have gone to university and got her degree and built a successful career? Or maybe she would have married the man of her dreams, built a house and reared a family in the warmth and glow of a loving and caring relationship.

I sat up and wiped the tears from my face. Looking at the crucifix leaning against the wall on my locker, I said a prayer. "Father, God in heaven, have I not suffered enough for you? What more is there that you want from me? If you want my life, then take it now, because I do not want to live like this. But if you don't want my life, then give it back to me. I don't want to be alone with only the horrors of my past for companions. Please God, send me a man I can love, a real man with a real heart who will love me and not judge me, who will care for me and never hurt me and who will understand my past and be patient with me while I try to come to terms with it."

I finished the prayer and, still sobbing, I lay my head on the pillow and fell asleep.

I had no work the following day and it was just as well. I must have been really exhausted because I did not wake up until eleven o'clock. After I had showered I decided I would get out of the flat for a while and head into the city centre to chill out. Maybe I could find a job while I was there. I also had an appointment to meet some friends later that evening for dinner – it was their treat, to thank me for some help and advice that I had given them to process some work permit papers. My experience of working in the recruitment agency came in useful sometimes.

When I got to O'Connell Street, for no particular reason I decided to have a look around Eason's bookstore. I did not expect this man who had his head turned away from me to grab my hand accidentally as he reached blindly for the same book that I had just put my hand on. It startled me and I let the book drop. The book dropped a few more times as we both tried to retrieve it and I felt a rush of embarrassment as we bumped heads in what can only be described as a comedy of errors. But when this man spoke to me, joking and trying to make light of the situation, I could see by his face that it was not just me who was embarrassed.

Although his manner was confident, his shyness was clear to see and in a strange way it eased my own embarrassment. I actually smiled when he made a joke about buying me some coffee, which was something I would never dream of doing with someone I did not know. Again, for some reason I cannot explain, I agreed to go with him and have that coffee, such was my instant comfort with him. He had a wonderful smile that radiated warmth and charm and probably the saddest eyes I had ever seen in my life. They were beautiful big blue eyes, but the sadness within them was hiding a pain that must have been torturous.

As we sat over the coffee in the hotel and I chatted with Noel before telling him my story, I could see from his face and his manner that he was a kind, cultured and a very intelligent man. But his face also betrayed his inner self and I could see that behind the smile he was full of problems. But as I sat with him, looking at him, comfortable in and enjoying his company, I remembered my prayer of the previous night and I wondered if God had finally listened to me. I did not reveal this to Noel as I brought my story to a close in the flat; it was much too personal and over-presumptive at this time.

16

Consummation of a Dream

Noel

"That is one hell of a story, Luz," I said, enthralled by her and her tale. "That's not a life story, it's several lives that you've lived. You're an incredible woman to have survived all of that."

I meant every word of it. Her honesty was both refreshing and astounding. There were no corners to this woman; what you saw was what you got. As each minute spent with her ticked by I wanted her more and more. Luz had told me so much that some of it was only sinking in now. For instance, I could hardly believe looking at Luz that she had five children. Never in a million years would I have guessed that she had a daughter in her twenties.

The kettle went on again. As Luz walked to the kitchen counter, she said, "Okay, Noel, you know everything about me now. So how about you – I am sure that you have an interesting story to tell?" *Interesting* was not the word I would have chosen – *disturbed*, *troubled* or *problematic* would have been my choice – but if interesting was on offer, then I would gladly accept it. And so at one o'clock in the morning, with Luz sitting on the floor beside me, both of us drinking tea, I told Luz the story of my life from beginning to end. I left no stone unturned, reciprocating and giving her the same respect that she had shown me.

When I had finished, Luz said, "I knew when we chatted earlier today, Noel, that your life was full of problems, but I feel sad for you and the hurt you have experienced, because you are a good man. We all make mistakes but you don't deserve all those problems in your life." She spoke with such warmth and feeling that it really touched me. I wondered what strange forces were at play that day that had brought this wonderful woman into my life.

Luz looked at her watch and said in surprise, "Noel, I can't believe it, but it's already four o'clock." I couldn't believe it either; we had started talking in Luz's flat at half past ten. Where had five and a half hours gone? "You are welcome to stay, Noel. I don't have a spare room, but you can sleep on the sofa or I'll make you up a bed on the floor if you like."

I could see that she was embarrassed by not having something more comfortable to offer me. "The floor will be fine, Luz – I'm used to sleeping on the floor. Anyway, I'm so tired at the moment I think I could probably sleep standing up!"

Indeed, I was used to sleeping on the floor. When I had arrived in my mother's house from Tipperary, it was already a full house. Gregory, the son of my sister Lorraine and her husband Paul, is autistic and one portion of the house was allotted for his needs. My youngest sister Christine and her husband Joe's daughter, Rachel, was born with disabilities and another portion of the house was dedicated to her needs. So when I had arrived with my bits and pieces, I was adding to an already-crowded dwelling. But my mother, Margaret Donegan, like the wonderful woman and mother that she is, had no hesitation in giving the front room of her house over to me. I was now living in this room, with a sleeping bag on the floor for my bed.

As I settled myself on the floor and closed my eyes, inviting sleep, I smiled and thanked whoever or whatever it was "up there" for inspiring me and guiding me into that bookstore.

I opened my eyes to the new day. Just for a moment I was startled as my brain made sense of the unfamiliar surroundings. *It wasn't a dream after all*, I thought to myself as I lay there smiling, remembering the events of the previous day. But I *had* been dreaming while I slept and when I finally managed to recall the details it took me by surprise.

I had been dreaming about my father. In the years since his death, I can recall only one other occasion when I dreamed about him. On that occasion, it was that bittersweet dream that I am sure anyone who has ever lost a loved one could tell you about. The euphoric moment when you once again lay eyes upon them, hold them and bathe in the pure joy that they are not gone, they were never gone. You surrender eagerly to the delusion that this is real and that the sad reality was just a bad dream. But reality will not be dismissed so easily. Fervent and unrelenting, it seeks you out; it will not be denied. It finds you and in the waking moment it takes hold and mercilessly drags you back to its domain. It is a horrible moment. Instantly your dream is shattered and once again you relive the sorrow and feel the loss you so desperately tried to bury some place deep inside yourself. Thinking about it now, perhaps that is why I did not recall dreaming of my dad. Maybe somehow, subconsciously, I managed to suppress the desire and in so doing save myself from the heartache of reliving the loss of that man whom I loved so dearly.

But now, as I recalled my new dream, I was not sad or overcome by feelings of loss. In fact, it was the complete opposite. Maybe the dream was just a flight of fancy or a tired and overactive mind trying to make sense of an extraordinary day's events. Whatever the reason, I could not deny the significance. I dreamed I was standing in a bookstore; I had just purchased a book and, on turning its pages, I stopped on one which contained a picture of my father!

"Did you sleep well, Noel?" Luz asked as she emerged from her bedroom, her question snapping me out of my thought.

"Yes, I was very comfortable, thanks. I slept like a baby."

I was delighted to be in her company again. Yesterday I had left my house vowing to make it the first day of the rest of my life. As I picked my bedding up from the floor, looking over at Luz who was preparing some breakfast, it was certainly living up to my promise.

We chatted over breakfast and I explained that I had to go to Tipperary for a meeting, which would also be a chance for me to see the kids. I told Luz how much I had enjoyed our day and that if she did not mind I would love to see her again when I got back. "I would really like that, Noel," was her welcome reply.

Thankful for the travel pass I received as part of my disability payment, I boarded the train at Heuston Station. The good thing about travelling by train is that it gives you time to think. Most of my train journey to Tipperary was spent thinking about Luz and what was happening in my life. *Could this be really happening?* I asked myself. I tried to comprehend the craziness of what had happened in the previous twenty-four hours and the feelings I had towards a woman who, until the day before, I never even knew existed. But, crazy and irrational as it all seemed, I could not deny that what had happened had really happened.

As for my feelings for Luz, perhaps it was good that I had to be away for a few days like this; it would put them to the test and allow me some time to reflect. Everything about Luz seemed so right. She was beautiful, intelligent and, from what I had experienced, she appeared to be a good-living woman with a really understanding and kind heart.

But it was not Luz I had concerns about; it was me. So much of Luz's story was one of abuse and disappointment, suffered mostly at the hands of and because of men. I wanted to be sure that, before I acted on the feelings that were developing in my heart and because of my past life and my current circumstances, I would not be adding another name to her list of disappointments. What did I have to offer her but more problems? It appeared to me that she'd already had her fair share of them.

This was the last thing I had expected to happen in my life. With the break-up of my marriage and the fallout that had ensued, involvement with women was not high on my priority list. But, despite myself, it happened. I reasoned that if the feeling was so strong in the face of my reservations, then there had to be something special happening here. What else could explain two strangers from other sides of the world meeting by chance and, within hours, both of them telling each other their life stories?

We called each other and sent texts over the course of the three days that I was away, every communication adding a little more strength to the bond that was developing between us. By the end of the third day I was really anxious to see Luz again. It had been great to see the kids and as I left Tipperary and headed back to Dublin I wished that I could have put them in my pocket and brought them back with me. The train was pulling into Dublin's Heuston station when I sent Luz a text and asked her if it would be okay if I called in to see her. Her flat was only a five-minute walk from the station.

Luz

When I received Noel's text I could not understand my feelings. I had tried not to think about Noel too much while he was away; I dared not hope that he was the man I had asked for in my prayer. Refusing to think about

Noel as anything other than a really great guy I had met prevented me investing anything of myself into a crazy hope and would lessen the disappointment in case I never saw him again. But now, as I read his text, I knew he had come back to me and I was so excited at the prospect of seeing him again. Maybe, just maybe, I could start to hope.

I replied to his text, telling him it was good to know he was back and that I'd be happy if he called in to see me. He could easily have knocked on my door unannounced but I really appreciated his manners and the way he did not take me for granted. When Noel arrived at the flat I introduced him to a Filipino friend of mine who was paying me a visit. The three of us chatted for a while. I was always glad to see friends and loved to cook for and entertain for them; but this was different. Now all I could think about my friend was, *I wish he would stop talking and leave so that I can chat with Noel on my own.* I started cleaning up the counter and the kitchen and eventually, much to my relief, he got the hint and left.

When he was gone Noel came over to me, kissed me on the cheek and gave me a hug. "It's great to see you again, Luz. You know, I really missed you." It was so nice and all very polite and proper, but I was not used to such uninhibited displays of affection. Thinking back, I must have stood there like a stick because I don't remember hugging Noel back. "I missed you too, Noel. I was very happy when you asked to call on me," I replied, recovering from my impression of a plank of wood.

When I had made up something for us to eat we sat on the floor and Noel told me all about his trip, seeing the kids and his business meeting. It was so easy for us to talk to each other, so easy for us to express our feelings – and it was, oh, so nice to be in the company of a man who made me feel safe! We laughed so much that night; we joked, played darts and had a really great time together. I tried to remember the last time that I had felt that way. But I couldn't remember, because I had never felt like this before in my life.

I had never been in the company of a man whom I wanted to be with because I liked him. I simply loved being in Noel's company and I wondered if this is what it feels like to be falling in love. This feeling of excitement that made my heart race and my breath quicken every time Noel held my hand or came so close that I could feel his breath on my neck – was this what I had longed for and been denied all of my life?

It must have been around one o'clock in the morning when we decided that it was time to sleep. Noel had asked me to spend the next day with him and so once again I prepared a bed for him on the floor.

Noel

I watched Luz as she prepared the bed and my eyes devoured her. I was helplessly in love. Impossible and impractical as it seemed, I could not deny or ignore those feelings, as to do so would be to ignore this most beautiful gift that had been bestowed upon my life.

When Luz had the bed made she walked over to me and said, "Goodnight, Noel. I have really enjoyed myself today and I hope you had a good time too?"

I took her hand in mine, held it tightly, and looked into her beautiful brown eyes. "Luz, just being here with you and seeing you again is enjoyment enough for me." Still holding her hand in mine, I put my arm around her waist and kissed her cheek while whispering into her ear, "Goodnight, Luz." She turned her head slightly and our eyes met again. Holding the gaze, we said nothing. Our eyes did the talking as we let go of our fear and revealed to each other the depth of our desire.

I slept on the floor that night, but not alone. There was honesty in our hearts and a total abandonment of all the bad that we had experienced in our lives which made that night magical and conjured into being a love that would fill our sails and sustain us on our voyage to a place where dreams are made. We had found each other and in each other we found the strength to challenge and become more than our pasts had shaped us to be.

But I found more than Luz when I moved the following night from the floor into the bedroom. Turning on my side as I slept, my hand went under Luz's pillow and I jumped when I felt the point of something very sharp sticking into my finger.

"Jesus, what's that?" I said as some blood trickled from a small cut. Luz looked at me, shocked and then embarrassed as she reached under the pillow and pulled out a knife. "What in the name of God is that doing there?" I asked, more than a little surprised.

"Well, you know, the first night that you slept in the flat, Noel, I didn't really know you, so to be honest I slept very little that night and when I did sleep it was with my hand under the pillow holding onto the knife."

I could see by the way she was looking at me that she didn't know how I was going to react. "That is very disappointing, Luz," I said, looking as serious as I possibly could.

"But why are you disappointed, Noel?"

"It's very disappointing, Luz, because I thought you had that knife under your pillow so that you could rape me!" I replied, trying to restrain my laughter.

Luz instantly shot back, "Hmm . . . I think I could have done that to you with a paper knife, Noel." And we both laughed ourselves silly.

I was so happy that Luz could laugh like this now about a topic that had such personal memories for her. We were breaking down barriers and we were doing it with laughter.

But the laughing did not stop there. The following morning when I woke up with Luz snuggled in closely to me, she said, "Can I ask you something, honey?"

"Of course you can, sweetheart, ask me anything you like."

"Are you gay, Noel?"

I nearly choked as I gulped a sharp intake of air, not believing what she had just asked me. "Was it that bad?" I replied, trying to recover my composure and my deflated ego.

Luz started laughing uncontrollably. "No, that's not what I meant, honey." Tears ran down her cheeks as she laughed hysterically at my reaction and the look on my face. "You told me you worked as a hairstylist. Well, in the Philippines only gay men work as hairstylists, so I was just wondering if you were gay or a double blade!" She was enjoying teasing me now.

"Double blade? What in the name of God is double blade?" I asked, the laughter now infectious.

"You know, honey – cuts both ways." With that I just cracked up and we laughed until my stomach was sore.

That's the way it was with Luz; there was no processing time between whatever thought came into her head and its arrival on her tongue. It made for some hilarious moments and, later, I would often cringe when we were in company as I never quite knew what she was going to come out with next.

We spent the next few days as if we were the only two people in the world. We were lost in each other and immersed in the joy of our new-found love. It seemed as though time had stood still for us. But time stands still for no one and a phone call from my sister Lorraine reminded me that there was another universe outside of our world with its population of two.

"Jesus, Noel, where are you? Where have you been for the last few days? We've been worried about you." Her voice shook, but more from relief than anger. I apologised to Lorraine and my mother for worrying them like that. They knew I had been battling with depression and were only too aware of where it had led me before. When I hadn't returned home or made a phone call to them they had feared the worst.

"Lorraine, there is someone I want you and my mother to meet. When you do, it will explain everything to you."

The following day I introduced Luz to my family. From the very first moment that my family met Luz, they loved her. They could see all of the qualities that I had seen in her and they could see how happy I was with her. My mother, who is a very shrewd judge of character, called me aside. "Luz is a lovely person, Noel. Don't ever lose her." With my arm around my mother I smiled and my smile told her everything she needed to know.

During the course of our visit, Luz asked to see my room. Looking at the sleeping bag on the floor she shook her head in surprise. "Oh, Noel, I didn't know! I thought you were just joking with me when you said you were used to sleeping on the floor." She gave me a big hug and said, "These are the things that make us stronger and these are the things we should never forget."

I loved her for that; she loved me for myself, for there was nothing else. It was such a far cry from what I was used to. In the past all that seemed to matter were the possessions and the only semblance of love was when I produced them. It was always about what was on show and never about what lay beneath; but with Luz it was so different. She was not impressed by possessions or shows of wealth. What mattered to Luz was the person and the truth within. I realised now that I had been conditioned over the years to buy affection and not to value myself for what I had to offer. But Luz was changing all that. She taught me to value myself for who I was and told me that the love we shared was worth more to her than any possession I could ever buy her.

Luz met all of my family including my mother, my elder brother Sonny, my sisters Lorraine, Maria and Christine, and the youngest member of the family, my brother Darren. Luz was really impressed by the closeness of my family and the way that we cared for and supported each other.

"You're all so easy to get on with and everyone is so kind and welcoming to me." Luz was drawing a comparison to her previous experiences.

"Thank you, sweetheart, it makes me proud to hear you say that. But they love you because you're also easy to get along with and a good and kind person." I was referring to the way Luz was spending time to massage my disabled niece Rachel, and the time she gave to Gregory, my autistic nephew, who absolutely loved her.

With a tear in her eye, Luz replied, "You know, Noel, I have never been happier in my whole life than I am right now being with you and a part of this family."

The time we were spending together was pure bliss. We were like kids who had been let loose in the candy store and we were gorging ourselves on happiness. We sang, we danced – well, Luz danced and I stepped on her toes – we went jogging and practised martial arts in the Phoenix Park. Freed from the lies and released from the pressures of supporting those lies, I felt I was finally finding myself again and I liked who I had found. I was getting a second chance with Luz and she wanted the real me, not what anyone else thought I should be.

I called Luz's flat the Philippines Embassy. It seemed that every stray Filipino somehow managed to find their way there looking for help. At first it was amusing and I loved her willingness to try to help anyone that she could, but after a while it became clear to me that some of these people were taking advantage of her kindness. At three, or maybe four o'clock in the morning, her mobile would ring, waking her from her sleep with a call from someone that she had never met, asking if they could sleep in the flat, as they had just arrived at the airport from the Philippines. Luz's mobile number had been passed around like it was a personal helpline from one person to the other but without any regard for Luz or the times that they were calling and waking her. But what really upset me was that, having received Luz's help, none of them could remember her after they had got what they wanted. A simple thank you means so much and demonstrates a little respect.

We spoke about it and Luz agreed with my view but she just hated to say no, even though she knew that it was becoming too much. That was Luz – a wonderful, compassionate woman, but so naïve when it came to dealing with people who didn't have her interests at heart. But it was okay – I was no longer naïve and I would bring balance to her generosity.

It came to a head at three o'clock one morning when the mobile rang with someone looking for help, followed thirty minutes later by someone actually ringing the doorbell. Taking the mobile from Luz, I said, "Sorry, sweetheart, I really hope you're not going to be angry with me for this, but someone has to do it." I opened the phone, took the SIM card out and flushed it down the toilet. I put my arm around Luz's shoulder and said, "Now, let's go back to bed and get a decent night's sleep."

Laughing, Luz looked up at me. "Now, why didn't I think of that?"

I really enjoyed meeting Luz's friends and learning about Filipino culture. One lady in particular made a big impression on me. Pilar Kavanagh is a Filipina, married to James Kavanagh, and she has lived in Ireland for over thirty years. Together with her son Jade, she would often visit us in the flat and she never came empty-handed. If it was not rice, then it was fish or something else for us to eat. She is a wonderful lady, small in stature but with a very big heart, and she has become one of our dearest friends.

We had been surviving on my disability payment and the last of Luz's money that she had received from the sale of her tricycles in the Philippines. With the money nearly gone and social welfare payment not worth talking about, we needed to do something fast to turn our financial situation around and build a foundation on which to build our life. Uppermost in our thoughts were our children and we wanted to get ourselves into a position to provide for them.

Luz's idea for importing the health food supplements seemed to offer us the best chance of achieving this goal, so we put all of our energies into securing the permissions from the various government agencies. Day by day, we made a little more progress, but because the supplier was based in Malaysia, there was a big time difference involved when communicating with them. The consequence of this was that, by day we worked on our business and marketing plans and by night and into the early hours of the morning we communicated with the supplier. It was a pretty exhausting schedule.

With all of the government agencies, we would get so far and then we would hit a brick wall. The problem was that all of the ingredients in the products and their recommended daily allowances needed to be verified by independent scientific analysis. On hearing from us that we needed this data, the supplier in Malaysia promised to send it to us immediately by email. True to their word, the data arrived the following day, but as Luz and I read through it we noticed that, although it was a scientific analysis of the products, it appeared it had been conducted by their own laboratories. We sent it to the relevant government agencies anyway, but their conclusion was the same as ours; it was not "independent" analysis and they could not accept it.

Over the coming months, despite repeated requests we still did not receive independent analysis from Malaysia. Without this information we could not move forward, so we made the decision to carry out our own analysis and hired an EU-approved scientist to do the tests on the products. Within a few weeks the results were back and they were not what we had been hoping for. Not only were quantities of the ingredients excessively high, way outside what was acceptable for importation into the EU, but if they were consumed by anyone with a particular allergy to them, it could be very dangerous indeed.

Although we were totally deflated by this news and with all of our hard work amounting to nothing, it could have been much worse. Our business plan had been submitted to the bank and we were poised to purchase a large quantity of the product with a loan secured by guaranteed sales that we had lined up. Had we drawn down this loan prior to the analysis and purchased this stock, not only would we have been deflated but we would also have been very heavily in debt.

However, the question remained: where did we go from here? Our plan to distribute this product was supposed to be the answer to our financial problems and we had invested a lot of our hopes in it. Now it lay in tatters at our feet. Luz was particularly depressed over the news. She had worked her back off and spent a lot of money processing the various documents that were required for the business. Luz felt very let down by this company in Malaysia, who had given her guarantees that the product would conform to EU standards.

Embarrassment was then added to disappointment for me when my son sent me a text looking for money and I had nothing to send him. I had spent my social welfare payment, such that it was, on food and, because we had been meeting with the banks for the health foods, I also needed to buy some new clothes to make myself presentable. Luz used her money to send my son what he needed. "There is no need to be embarrassed, Noel, I will always treat your kids as my kids and I know you would do the same for me."

I really appreciated Luz saying that and I knew that she really meant it but it was not how I wanted it to be. I did not want Luz to think that I was like the others and only interested in what I could get out of her.

A few weeks later it happened again and once again Luz was the one to send him what he needed. Because the kids were not living with me I was only getting a single person's allowance and there was never anything left over by the end of the week. Luz had a heart of gold and I loved her for it, but it still did not stop the embarrassment I felt when this happened.

I considered going back to work as a hairdresser but I knew in my heart that, because of my nervous breakdown and the anxiety I was experiencing in my life, I no longer possessed the tolerance or the patience required to do that job. It was fine working with Luz as we struggled to find solutions for our problems – we were a team and we understood each other – but I was not yet ready to re-enter mainstream employment. My injured mind could not handle it yet. Luz was still processing her business permission and a condition of that application was that she could not enter into any gainful employment. It was looking really bad for us and I began to worry about what was going to become of us.

17

Sad

If on a financial level our life was empty then, by comparison, on a relationship level we were abundant. It was obvious that we were meant for each other and that this relationship was going the distance, money or no money.

I suggested to Luz that perhaps I should meet my wife and the children to tell them about us; I did not want my children hearing about Luz and me from someone else. Luz agreed that it was a good idea and so I arranged to meet them in a coffee shop in Thurles. I did not feel comfortable to meet my wife in private, especially after what I had been accused of in the past. Luz felt it was not appropriate for her to be present at that meeting as it might be too much for the kids to handle at that time. So while I headed to the coffee shop, Luz went browsing about the shopping centre.

When my wife arrived with the kids, I arranged for my son and daughter to sit at a separate table so that I could speak privately with her first before I explained to the kids. It was sad to realise, as I sat across the table from her, that I felt nothing for this woman with whom I had spent more than twenty years of my life. It was not like me to feel that way about anyone, but the things that had now passed between us ensured that in this case I was definitely prepared to make an exception.

I started to tell her about Luz and me but as I did I could see her face redden and her blood starting to boil. I knew that look only too well. I knew what it meant and I knew what was coming next. "I can't believe this. I can't believe you are doing this to me!" Her voice rose up a notch, drawing not only the attention of the kids to us but also most of the coffee shop. She was getting into character as she prepared to play her well-rehearsed role of the injured party in the drama I knew she was about to orchestrate.

I smiled over at the kids to reassure them that everything was okay before I responded to her. "What is wrong with you? I told you a long time ago that we were finished. You accused me of the most horrendous acts, called the police to our home and tried to make me appear like a wife-beater in front of my son, denied your involvement in the money that we borrowed, tried to get a barring order issued against me, told me that I should have thrown myself under a train and you changed the locks on our house to keep me out! Is that your idea of foreplay?" I could not resist the sarcastic tone, such was the absurdity of her reaction. "I came here today out of what I can now see was a misguided courtesy to you, so that you would hear from my mouth about Luz and not from the mouth of some idle gossiper."

But she was not listening to me. I could read her like a book now and I watched as her eyes scanned the coffee shop. I could almost hear her brain working as it assessed how she could use the situation to her advantage. Acting almost hysterically, she said to me, "I need to get out of here after what you've just said to me. And you'd better drive me home with the kids, because I might crash the car and kill us all."

By now we were the centre of attention in the coffee shop and the kids were getting agitated. It appeared she was getting exactly what she wanted. She had her audience. The only thing everyone who was looking at us could hear and see were the sounds and actions of a supposedly distraught woman upset by what her estranged husband was saying to her and upsetting the innocent kids in the process. But I had not raised my voice, I had not upset the kids and I was not throwing the histrionics. No one knew what I had said, but I was the one who was looking bad again.

"I can't drive you home," I told her. "Luz is here in the shopping centre and I am not leaving her here and going back to the house with you. I will never put myself in that position again." This time I was calling her bluff.

"I don't care, she can come in the car, but just get me out of here, because if I drive that car I will kill the three of us." She got up from the table and continued what I can only describe as playacting. As ever when she could not get what she wanted, she resorted to her blackmailing technique. It was not how I wanted Luz to be introduced to my children but I had no choice. If I did not drive them home and then I heard on the news that they were killed in a car crash, how could I live with that?

I called Luz on her mobile and asked her to join us. Luz was obviously reluctant but when she heard that I was worried for the kids' safety she understood my position. With Luz sitting in the back of the car beside the kids, I drove them back home. I had not even considered how Luz and I would get back to Thurles train station – all my attention and concern was focused on the kids and ensuring that they got home safely. If we had to, Luz and I would walk the four miles from the house back to the train station.

It was a very uncomfortable situation to be in and I could only begin to imagine how Luz and the kids must have felt, thrown together like that. But what choice did they have? This crazy scenario was all at my wife's request and I could not help but wonder, as I looked at the kids, that did she not consider how this might be impacting on them. Or was getting us all to do what she wanted all that mattered?

When we got to the house, we all went in. I wanted to be sure that the kids were settled and okay before we left. My son immediately ran upstairs to his bedroom and my daughter went into the conservatory while my wife went into the sitting-room. I was talking to my daughter while she played with her hamster when I suddenly heard my wife shouting, "Quick, quick! Phone for an ambulance! Get me a doctor!" I ran to see what was wrong. When I got there, Luz was standing beside the door to the room. "Noel, this is only a drama. As soon as I heard her calling out, I put my head inside the door to see what was wrong, and she laughed and stuck her tongue out at me." Luz was shaking her head in disbelief at what she had just witnessed.

Although I was really annoyed at my wife's antics – how they appeared to have been planned and executed to upset the kids and to make Luz and me look bad in their eyes – I also said a silent *Thank you God* to myself. At last someone else had witnessed at first hand what I had been subjected to for so many years, with such damaging consequences for me. It is so difficult and frustrating when you are constantly trying to justify your life, trying to explain why you did what you did or are the way that you are, but it's even worse when you have to defend yourself against lies to people who have already tried you and decided you are guilty. But now Luz had seen with her own two eyes just how manipulative and downright calculating this woman could be. At last I had someone who could say, "Yes, I have seen and know exactly what Noel is talking about. He is not making it up; it's real." The threat about crashing the car, it seemed, was just a ploy to get us here so she could play out her drama.

Now that I knew this to be the case, I also knew that we needed to get out of there before she upped the ante. I had learned that when it came to a perceived crying mother and upset kids, there was only ever going to be one winner in that scenario. "We need to get out of here, sweetheart, in case she thinks of doing something else," I said to Luz.

However, first I needed to know that the kids, who were now very upset, were going to be all right. I phoned a neighbour and asked her if she would come over to the house and stay with the kids when we left. The neighbour arrived but I had not considered what she might have been told about me since I had left. Pointing her finger at

Luz, she said, "Don't you get involved with Noel, you don't know him."

Luz just looked at her but did not reply. Then, taking my arm tightly in hers, she said to me, "Take no notice of her, Noel, because I'm certainly not. What gives her the right to say that or think that she knows you? She is only a neighbour – what does she know about your life except the poison that she has been fed about you? I am sure that you don't know what goes on between her and her husband."

And as we walked out of the house to take our lift back to the train station, Luz turned to me and said, "I have had a hard life, Noel, and had some terrible things done to me, but this is the first time in my life I have ever experienced anything like that. Now I have some idea of what you have gone through." She kissed me on the cheek as she went on, "I am so sorry for you, honey."

Luz

When we got back to the flat I could see that Noel was still very upset and thinking about the kids. Incidents like that were not good for Noel at all and I was afraid he would fall back into a depression. He was already heart-broken and distraught from not seeing his kids. Many times I would find him with tears in his eyes when a memory crossed his mind or something happened that reminded him of them. If only they could see this wonderful man at those times, or hear how he called out their names in his sleep, often with tears running from his closed eyes, they would never question his love for them.

It was not their fault but it was not his fault either. He had done nothing that warranted such treatment. The proof of this was very obvious to me. How could Noel suddenly seem so bad in the eyes of his children at the very same time that his marriage broke up? How could he suddenly become a bad father at the same time as he left their mother? The answer seemed obvious to me: perhaps they had been encouraged to see him in this way. I am sure it was done indirectly but the results were still devastating for Noel. To my mind, it is wrong for any parent to stand back and say nothing while their child forms an obviously misguided opinion about someone or something in their life. Sometimes what we don't say can do as much or more damage as what we do say. Silence is not golden, despite what the song says.

It seemed that the children had formed a misguided view that to see their father would in some way be an act of betrayal to their mother, with whom they had to live and share a house. It seemed obvious to me that this view had not been discouraged. The fathers of my children had treated me horrifically and, had I wanted to, I could have easily discouraged my children from seeing them ever again. But I would never use my children in that way or use them as a means to hurt anyone. I have far more respect for them and myself than to do that. After the death of my dad, I knew only too well how hard it can be on a child growing up not to have a father in their life. Nothing can replace the love of a good father or a good mother. I had no choice: death stole my father away from me. But for any mother or father to be the cause of depriving a child of that special love that only a parent can give to my mind can never be justified.

It broke my heart to watch Noel when he was sad like this. I remember one night we were watching a football match. Manchester United were playing Chelsea and I noticed Noel was wiping tears from his eyes. Noel is a Chelsea fan and they were losing the game 0-1. "Is it that sad?" I teased him, thinking he really takes his football very seriously. But it was not like that; he had been remembering how he and his son, who is a Manchester United fan, would watch these games together. The memory was so sad for him.

Another time during Christmas we were watching the film *Chitty Chitty Bang Bang* and in the movie a little girl with blonde hair sings a song called "Truly Scrumptious". Halfway through the song, Noel got up and went into the kitchen. When there was no sign of him returning, I went to the kitchen to see if he was okay. I found him there sobbing his heart out. The song was one of the first his daughter had learned to sing in her stage school.

If there was an intention to break Noel's heart by depriving him of his children, then it had well and truly succeeded. If anyone could be happy for that, then all I can say is, God forgive them. Noel lived for his kids; it was so obvious that he adored them and they were the main driving force in his life. I felt so sorry for Noel, but there was nothing I could do except comfort him, let him see how much I loved him. Hard as it was to do, I told Noel that he had a choice to make. He could continue as he was and have his heart torn apart every day by the grief, until all that was left of him was the part that was to be buried. Or he could look into himself and see the love he had given his children, and hold that place somewhere inside and go there when he missed them and be happy in the knowledge that this is what he had given them.

I told Noel that it was important for him to live his life and to be the best that he could be. His children would be adults someday and, with the insight of an adult, maybe they would question their motives and see another truth. Here was the most wonderful man, loving, caring, understanding and selfless to a fault in every aspect of his life, and yet life had been so cruel to him. Where is the justice, I wondered?

Noel had accepted me for who I was, without question. With every passing day his love and understanding erased another part of my dark past and replaced it with the light of hope and the promise of a future. Noel loved with a passion and through his understanding and gentleness made me happy in ways I thought I could never know. Separate we were vulnerable and prey to the consequences of our pasts, but together and in each other we had discovered a strength that no one or nothing would ever breach.

Noel

Through the mediation of the family support services in Tipperary, I managed to arrange a meeting with my son under their supervision in Thurles. I cannot describe how excited I was to have this opportunity to see my son, but I had no sooner agreed to it than my wife was interfering and imposing her conditions on it. One of the mediators called me and said that my wife did not want Luz at the meeting. Luz immediately said to me, "Tell them that's no problem, honey. I will never be used as a reason why you cannot see your children." We agreed to her condition, but I imposed a condition of my own. I told the mediator that I did not want my wife present; this meeting was for my son and me and in light of the recent incidents I did not want to be in the same room as her.

Luz and I travelled down to Tipperary and Luz waited outside for me while I had the meeting with my son. It was obviously great to see him again, if a little strange to see people there as if we needed a referee, but whatever it took, I was willing to go there if it meant he was back in my life again. The meeting gave us some time to talk together but, more importantly, it gave my son a platform to express some of the things that he was feeling about the break-up of his parents' marriage. He told me that he understood that I was with Luz now, but that he needed some time before he could get comfortable with the idea. I told him that I fully understood what he was saying and that if he wished to keep meeting me on my own for a while, it would not be a problem. Luz only wanted what was the best for him. When the meeting was over I gave my son a watch that Luz and I had bought for his birthday, but he refused to accept it. The meeting, however, was a great success and we scheduled the next one for a few weeks later.

Luz was absolutely delighted when I told her how the meeting had gone and she remarked how happy I looked. I told Luz that my son and I would be having the meetings on a regular basis and of his wish to continue seeing me on my own for a while. As usual Luz was a tower of strength, as I knew she would be. Luz had no problem with any of this; her main priority was for my son and me to have a proper father-and-son relationship again.

It was all going just a little too smoothly, though. Just before our next meeting was due to take place, I received a call from the mediators. There was a new condition my wife wanted to impose. She now wanted to be present at my meeting with my son, a condition she knew very well I could never accept. To me it appeared obvious that my last meeting had gone too well for her liking and now she wanted to impose a condition that she must have known was unacceptable and could only result in sabotaging the progress that had been made. To me it was selfish, cynical and unacceptable that she should interfere like that. She had my son to herself every day of the week and now, on this one occasion when I had a chance to see him for one hour in a couple of weeks, she wanted to interfere in it and destroy it. I could not accept what I perceived as an ultimatum and told the mediators so.

The following day I got a call from the mediators saying that the meeting was off if I would not agree, and that it was also my son's wish that his mother be present. Again, as had been the case throughout my marriage, it felt like I was being emotionally blackmailed. This time the choice I was being given was to see her and my son together or not to see my son at all. I could not understand it. If she was concerned about our son's welfare then I wondered why she would interfere in the meeting. What was wrong with me seeing my son on my own? When I asked the question, no one gave me an answer and I was left to form my own reasons as to the motives of her request.

I refused her demands and that was an end to me being able to see my son. It was cruel and heartless and I really hated her interference and what it had done. I wondered how she could sleep at night knowing that her unreasonable conditions had succeeded in depriving her son of the love of a father and that father of the love of his son.

18

The Card

Luz

With our financial crisis worsening and unable to pay the rent on the flat, we had no alternative but to move in with Noel's mother and Lorraine. I couldn't help but feel embarrassed imposing on Noel's family, as they had already been so good to me. I felt guilty landing myself on top of them and adding another body to an already very full house, but I had no need to as they were so under-standing and welcomed me with open arms.

I had not just found the love of my life in Noel but through him I had become part of a family who really loved me, and they showed it to me every day. Lorraine, Maria and Christine called me their sister and Noel's mother became a mother to me; I even called her "Mammy". The love and kindness I received from this family overwhelmed me and I felt so blessed to be a part of them. Without their love and support, God only knows what would have happened to us. I was so proud and excited to call my children and tell them of the wonderful man in my life and his fantastic family who loved me and respected me so much. I never had to hide anything from Noel's family and they never hid anything from me. They accepted me and loved me for who I was.

Not having to pay rent for a flat took a huge amount of the pressure away from us and we could breathe again. Mammy or Lorraine never once made us feel uncomfortable in that house. In fact, it was the very opposite; there was nothing that was too much trouble for them in their efforts to help us. However, I knew that it hurt Noel's pride to have to impose on them. He often used to say, "I should be the one caring for and looking after my mother, not the other way around." But he was giving so much to his mother that he could not see.

Mammy would often talk to me if she got me on my own. "You know, Luz, since Noel has been with you, we have our old Noel back. We had lost him for so long and he used to be so stressed and distracted, but now he is back to who he used to be." It made me so proud when Mammy said that to me and to feel that I had played a part in making them happy with the way Noel was now.

Noel and I had found each other and in each other we had found personal happiness and love. But now we needed to find a way to stand on our own two feet. Noel was forty-two years old and I was thirty-eight. If we were going to do something with our lives and for our future, we needed to do it now. Time was not on our side. What that something was we still needed to figure out, but I was confident that, together, we would find a way to achieve success and change our lives.

The alarm on the mobile phone went off, disturbing the silence and signalling the start of a new day. I stretched my limbs in preparation for getting up from the air bed. The aches and pains that I felt throughout my body told me that the bed had once again deflated during the night and the cold draughty air that crept in under the door had played upon my body.

I later found a solution to this problem by elevating our bedding from the floor, placing it on top of the office desk in the corner of our room. This took us out of the draught and some extra pillows and padding created a mattress. Necessity really is the mother of invention. We would often laugh as we went to sleep, joking that at least we could say, in all truth and honesty, given the long hours that we were working, that we awoke every morning at our desk.

As the mobility returned to my joints, I turned to look at Noel and saw that he was looking at the mobile with a very glum expression on his face. "What's wrong, honey?" I asked anxiously, wondering what had caused this mood.

Noel

As I turned off the alarm on the mobile, I noticed the date: 19 April 2003. It was Lorraine's birthday and I had forgotten all about it. I felt bad enough when I realised that we did not have the money to buy her a present, but

I felt absolutely dejected when I realised we didn't even have the money to buy her a birthday card.

It was one of those revealing moments when you can't hide from the desperate nature of your situation and you despise yourself for who you are and for getting yourself in this state. "I hate this, Luz, I don't care if I have to go and sweep the streets tomorrow, but I am not living like this any longer," I told her, getting more depressed by the second.

Luz caressed my face and kissed me on the forehead. "It's okay, honey. Leave it to me – I have an idea."

So while I lay on the bed searching my brain for the answer to how we could turn our lives around and get us out of the hole we were in, Luz had got up and was sitting at the desk. For some unknown reason, she was tearing up magazines! I knew that I was feeling down and not in a particularly good mood but I thought that maybe she had gone mad.

"What in the name of God are you doing, sweetheart?" I asked, totally puzzled by her seemingly crazy actions.

"Just wait, honey, you will see in a little while."

Luz was totally immersed in what she was doing and did not want to lose her concentration. I left her to it while I tackled the punctured and deflated air bed to see if I could repair the leak that had left us sleeping on the floor last night.

Thirty minutes later, Luz called to me, "Honey, what do you think of this?"

She was holding a colourful patterned object in her hand and waving it in the air. When I looked closer and saw what she had made, I was absolutely speechless.

Somehow, Luz had transformed the pages of the magazine into elongated strips and woven these strips together to create a birthday card that, when opened, revealed a space to insert a greeting of your choice. It was a thing of beauty. The colours and the abstract patterns they produced created a work of art.

"That is truly amazing, sweetheart! I've never seen anything like it." I was smiling, so proud of Luz for what she had created. But I wanted to know more about this incredible piece of invention. "Please show me how you did that, sweetheart; I need to know how you put this together."

A spark of an idea had ignited in my brain.

Luz took me step-by-step through the process of making the card and I was in awe of her ingenuity and resourcefulness. It was absolutely ingenious.

That evening and throughout the course of Lorraine's birthday celebrations all that my mind could think about was "that card". I didn't know what it was yet, but there was something within it that was crying out to be discovered. A little probing tomorrow would make it give up its secrets.

The following day the buzz of excitement was still with me. "Sweetheart, we are going to lock ourselves in here for the next few days and I want us to explore the technique you used for making that extraordinary card yesterday. Let's see what we can make from paper using that technique; let's also explore if there are other techniques we can discover to produce different results and different objects."

Luz went on to explain that when she was younger she had made paper straws by rolling paper together in her hands and that she had then woven the paper straws together to make little baskets, but that the card was the first time she had ever thought of making paper strips. Well, yesterday may have been the first day but it was not going to be the last. We gathered up every spare magazine and newspaper in the house and prepared for our experiment.

The few days that we had set aside to explore this technique soon became a week, and the week became a few weeks until we had spent months on this task, challenging ourselves to create as many items as we could. More and more possibilities opened up to us as we discovered more and more techniques. We honed and developed the techniques that we had discovered until we were confident that we could make objects from any sort of waste paper. The finished objects were incredibly strong and of a quality that was good enough to sell. We had made cards, table mats and coasters, pencil cases, trinket boxes, picture frames, waste bins, mobile phone holders and even a pair of slippers!

Of course, we needed to source as many different types of magazines, newspapers and catalogues as possible in order to test our methods and compare the results from using the different quality papers. It must have looked hilarious as we went into Argos on a very regular basis taking their catalogues, as we were particularly satisfied with the colour patterns achieved using the paper from their catalogues. I had visions of Luz and me appearing on some CCTV footage on *Crimeline* and being described as the phantom catalogue snatchers. Nowhere was safe from our paper-snatching activities. Leaflets and flyers in supermarkets we bagged by the dozens. We laughed ourselves silly as we imagined the manager rubbing his hands in delight at the expected response from the seemingly incredible uptake to his promotional leaflets.

My brother Sonny was a great help at this time. He would often drop in to us with ink for the PC, stationery, envelopes and other material for our samples and presentations. Sonny's contribution was very welcome.

This was a very exciting time and there was a real air of expectation about what we might be able to achieve with what we were discovering and inventing if only we could get it right. With the environment a very hot topic and recycling now a buzz word, I knew we were on the cusp of something big.

We needed to refine our techniques even further so that we could be assured at all times of the consistency of the work. If we could guarantee consistency then we could replicate and mass-produce. We set about creating and inventing tools that would give us this consistency and in so doing make the whole process much easier. We had been thinking all along that we would create these items from various types of waste paper and attempt to sell them as one-off pieces. If that proved to be successful we would try to find a way to mass-produce them and sell them into retail outlets. The plan was sound but it had one major flaw. If we were to mass-produce, it would require finance – a hell of a lot of finance – and no one was going to lend us money, certainly not with our credit history.

Then, as I was making a new tool to help us with the

work, the eureka moment happened. It would flip what we were doing totally on its head and give us a real chance to commercialise what we had discovered. We had been going about this entirely the wrong way. The tools we had invented, the techniques, the thrill and enjoyment of making something amazing from waste paper – *this* was the product. Instead of selling the items made by using the tools and techniques that we had invented, we would instead sell the tools and techniques so that people could make items from waste paper for themselves!

It is so hard to describe the feeling we experienced when we made this breakthrough. Until that moment, it was as if we were still unsure where we needed to go. At times it felt like we were swimming through muddy waters, always having to stop and check our position. But now the waters had cleared and we could see our final destination. Although it would be a difficult course to navigate, at least we knew where we wanted to go.

Our product would be an arts and crafts kit and we would aim to sell it within the toy and games industry. There was nothing out there in the marketplace like it and we were sure it would be a winner. If new product was the lifeblood of the toy industry, then we felt our product, which was so unique and so new, would give it a massive transfusion.

19

Gotta Get Through This

Luz and I were living and breathing the very same air every second of every day as we worked to sort out our life. It established a tremendously strong bond between us and we learned how to feed off and support each other's strengths and weaknesses. Having a dream is a wonderful thing but being able to share and pursue that dream with the person that you love and for them to play such a big part in it is a very fulfilling experience.

There were two routes we could take to try and commercialise our invention. We could try to secure funds to manufacture and sell the product ourselves; or we could try to license it. If we went the self-manufacturing route then we would require considerable backing to pay for tooling and manufacturing costs, not to mention marketing and distribution. It would require a huge effort and the risks would be high, but so would the rewards. Weighed against this was the licensing option. We could license the rights to a company who in turn would pay us a percentage of sales as a royalty. The advantage of going down this road was that they would pay all the costs for manufacturing, marketing and bringing the product to the market. But as they would be taking most of the risk, it meant that we would earn less money than if we manufactured it ourselves. There was a lot to think about, but one thing that we definitely needed to do before we could explore either option was to get our invention protected.

When we were confident that we had covered all of the angles, we met with Gearoid Schutte, a patent agent with Cruickshank & Co, a very well-respected and highly regarded company in the field of patents and intellectual property rights. Gearoid worked with us to draw up the patents and introduced us to Mary Rose O'Connor, who would help us on the trademark side of things. Gearoid is a lovely man to deal with and his expertise and professionalism were outstanding. His approach and interest in our product was very encouraging to Luz and me and it provided a welcome boost to our confidence.

Steve Lennon is the business development manager at Hasbro Ireland. Hasbro is one of the largest toy companies in the world. I have known Steve a long time, having probably annoyed the hell out of him on several different occasions, asking him for information and advice with some ideas I'd had in the past. All of these had come to nothing but, despite my now calling him again to pick his brains, he courteously invited Luz and me to the factory in Waterford to meet with him.

With Luz carrying the prototype, which at this stage was nothing more than the cardboard tools and rigs we had fashioned while in the house developing the invention, and me carrying a large box of samples, we headed to Heuston Station and on to Waterford. Luz was very excited going to Hasbro; it represented contact with the market we were hoping to enter and the first serious critique of our product. It felt really good to be doing something positive and it made us feel that at last we were exerting control over our lives.

Steve can only be described as a gentleman and is one of the few people whose opinion I really respect. Steve tells it to you like it is and he does not mince his words. If he thinks something is a waste of time, he will tell you so. From the moment Steve saw the items made from our craft kit, he said, "Guys, this is a winner. It's simply incredible how durable these items are and it's hard to believe they are made from paper." Steve's comments really encouraged us and we discussed with him what was involved if we were to try to manufacture the product ourselves. Hasbro Ireland provides turnkey manufacturing solutions which address customer needs from product concept through to delivery to market. If we were going to self-manufacture, then they were the people we wanted.

Steve, who is always the realist, pointed out that although he thought our product was fantastic, he wondered how on earth we would be able to finance the tooling and all the other costs involved, especially when we were broke. I explained that we were putting together a business plan and that we hoped the enterprise boards would weigh in behind us, especially considering that the product was so environmentally positive. Steve then made a suggestion. He had carried out some manufacturing for a company called Flair Leisure Products plc and, if we agreed, he would show our product to them and perhaps they might take a licence and contract Hasbro to manufacture it. This would mean we would have a royalty income and Hasbro would get to manufacture the product. It made a lot of sense to Luz and me, as we really had nothing to lose. We could still develop our business plan and follow the route we were taking for self-manufacture and if in the meantime we managed to license the product, so much the better. We gave Steve the go-ahead to show our product. Steve also said that he would do some estimates that would give us approximations for the cost of tooling and manufacture for our product. These figures would help greatly with our business plan, giving us a realistic handle on the manufacturing costs and a more concise idea as to the overall funds required to get our product off the ground. Our train journey home was filled with excited chatter about what we could do if all of this worked out. At last we could dare to dream of what might be.

On our arrival back in Dublin we discussed our next move. If we managed to get funds to manufacture, then that meant we would need to find customers to sell to. The government had launched an initiative called "The paper producers' responsibility for paper waste", which more or less meant that if the companies responsible for paper waste did not come up with solutions for dealing with that waste, then perhaps the government would impose a levy on them. Because our product was associated with recycling paper waste, it seemed that these companies should be our first port of call. Perhaps as part of their initiative for dealing with the problem they might contribute towards the manufacture of our product. We drew up a list which included Independent Newspapers, Eason's and Smurfit's. We also decided that, because of the green nature of the product, we would contact the Minister for the Environment and see if his department would row in behind us and offer us some form of grant aid. Our final port of call would be the environmental awareness officers of Dublin City Council to see if they could endorse or promote the product.

Despite making a bag and a serving tray to demonstrate what could be achieved by using our craft kit on their discarded newspapers instead of throwing them into the bin, Independent Newspapers showed no interest in our product. Smurfit's were next and seemed more promising. We met with their representative and he commissioned us to make 150 coasters for him with the Smurfit logo on them. He told us that he would use them as way of trying to generate interest in our product within the company. We were paid the princely sum one euro per coaster and it took several trips back and forth to their offices before we could collect it. We never heard anything further from them.

The environmental awareness officers loved the product and said they would definitely promote it through the schools in Dublin through their newsletter and would purchase some once it was manufactured and offer them as prizes for their competitions. They would also then suggest it to other councils around the country. This was great news; apart from it being a great way to promote the product through schools, it was another piece of positive data for our business plan.

The Department of the Environment was next. We lost count of how many times we tried to make an appointment with the Minister's office. We made phone calls, left messages and wrote letters but received no response. Fed up, we wrote a letter of complaint to the Taoiseach setting out our grievances with his Minister's office. A week later we had an appointment. We put forward our case for funding of the product based on its educational and environmental qualities but it was obvious by the body language of the official who we were talking to that he was only paying us lip service. It was galling. Every day Luz and I were watching this department's TV advertising campaign, "The Race against Waste", and here we were with a product which helped to tackle some of that waste in a fun, practical and educational manner, and they just dismissed us.

Eason's bookstores were next and in this instance we really did keep the best until last. We met with a gentleman called Colum Foley and showed him some items made from magazine waste. He loved them and on hearing that we were considering using Hasbro as our manufacturer, thereby ensuring the quality of the finished product, he said that he would be interested in giving us an order for thousands of units when the product was manufactured. We were delighted with this result. We had already sourced the manufacturer in Hasbro and through them established the costs per unit to produce the product and now, with the response we had received from Eason's, it proved that we had a market for our product and completed our business plan by proving we could sell in our first production run.

We spent the next few weeks putting all of this information into our business plan and making sure that all of the numbers added up. Without having a car, we depended on buses to get to our destinations, but without bus fare we could not always use them. I had a bus pass but its restrictions of use in the mornings and evenings meant that it was mostly of no use to me, as most of our travel had to be done during those peak times, and it was only of benefit to me. Lorraine and my mother would have given us bus fare without hesitation if we had asked, but they were already doing so much and we did not want to be bothering them all of the time. So we mostly hiked to our destinations, walking many miles carrying our large box of samples. Laughing at our situation and at just how poor we were, we would sing the Daniel Bedingfield song "I've Gotta Get Through This" as we walked from meeting to meeting. This was such a busy and exciting time and we were living by the sun, moon and stars.

Suddenly, without any warning, tragedy would pay a visit and leave not only Luz and me, but all of my family, totally devastated.

It was my sister Christine and her husband Joe's tenth wedding anniversary. Because of the special care required for their daughter Rachel, who had a disability which had not as yet been fully diagnosed but which had left her physically and mentally disabled, Joe and Christine had never gone away on their own to celebrate their wedding anniversaries. Rachel and Alison, Joe and Christine's other beautiful daughter, were very comfortable with my mother and Lorraine, so we were all delighted when Joe and Christine said that they would go to Brussels to celebrate their anniversary if my mother and Lorraine would mind the kids.

Joe and Christine are the most wonderful parents and dedicated themselves to providing Rachel with the best quality of life possible. They are fighters and would not accept anything but the best that Rachel could produce, constantly challenging her and themselves to pass the barriers others would have them accept. Until Rachel entered our lives, I never fully appreciated the gruelling schedule that is required to care for a child with special needs. My mother and Lorraine provided them with as much help as possible to try to make their life a little easier. It was not easy at times, because Lorraine's hands were already full managing Gregory, her autistic son. But like the great sisters that they are, they helped each other in every way possible to make a better life for these special children.

Luz and I have a huge amount of respect for Sarah, who is Lorraine and Paul's daughter and Gregory's sister. It must have been so difficult for her when so much time and effort was focused on Rachel and Gregory, but she was so mature and understanding of the situation that never once did I see her looking for attention. It was heartbreaking at times for Luz and me to watch them struggle, Lorraine, Christine and my mother doing everything they could to improve these children's lives.

Christine and Joe went to Brussels as planned. On the evening of 26 September 2003, Luz and I smiled with amusement as my mother and Lorraine took it in turns like a relay team to keep check on the kids sleeping upstairs. In the early hours of the morning of 27 September, Luz and I were awakened by the screams of my sister Lorraine calling my name as her husband Paul came rushing into our room. "Please, Noel and Luz, Lorraine needs help with Rachel." He was white as a sheet and almost speechless. Luz and I ran up the stairs where we saw Lorraine crying uncontrollably and shaking while standing over Rachel, who was on the bed, lying very still.

"Noel, I found Rachel face down between the two beds and when I lifted her up she was like this. I don't think she's breathing." Lorraine was in a terrible state.

Taking Rachel up in my arms, I ran downstairs and placed her on the floor. Luz and I worked on her, administering mouth-to-mouth and chest compressions as we attempted to resuscitate her while we awaited the ambulance. Our Lady's Hospital for Sick Children is a five-minute run from my mother's house, so Luz and I, not wanting to waste any time, wrapped Rachel in a blanket and, with her cradled in my arms, we both ran to the hospital. We had only gone a few yards when we spotted a van and flagged it down. All the time we were in the van we continued the mouth-to-mouth and the compressions until we got to the casualty department of the hospital.

As we placed Rachel into the hands of the doctors, she looked so peaceful that it was easy to imagine that she was just asleep. Luz and I were taken to a waiting area. After about twenty minutes the doctors came back with the news that Rachel had passed away. We were devastated.

I have faced some daunting tasks in my life but nothing can compare to the task that now lay ahead of me. With the phone in my hand, tears in my eyes and a lump in my throat, I made the call to my sister and her husband in Brussels to tell them that their beautiful daughter was dead. Nothing can ever prepare you for that or the feeling of self-loathing when after putting down the phone you know you have just delivered the news that has broken the hearts of people you love. Luz was a fantastic support throughout this difficult time and I don't know what we would have done without her.

Rachel was only with us for a little time, but that child touched every single one of us and made us better, more understanding people by being in our lives. She will never be forgotten.

20

Beyond Reason

We had been waiting on news from Steve Lennon on his dealings with Flair Leisure Products and when it arrived it was not the news we were hoping for. They had declined the product. It was disappointing, but at least we now knew that we needed to focus all our efforts on going down the self-manufacturing route.

Our business plan was complete but before we presented it to the enterprise boards or the banks, we decided to pass it by the accounts department of Deloitte and Touche, probably Ireland's largest professional services firm. It was gratifying and satisfying when, on collecting the business plan from them, they said they would not be charging us for the service as there was nothing they could do to improve on what we had submitted.

Confident in this knowledge, we made our appointment with the enterprise boards, little knowing that this would prove to be nothing more than an exercise in frustration.

We were bounced from one enterprise board to another, receiving comment that as a business we were either too large or too small to meet their qualifying criteria, depending on whom we spoke to. But it became insulting when an official of the city enterprise board held our business plan in his hand, felt the thickness of the plan between his fingers, and then rubbished it, criticising its size and content without ever turning a single page of the document. We left the meeting in disgust, but not before telling the official how insulting we found his behaviour and that if € 100,000 were put on the table for us now, we would not touch it if he was an example of what we would have to deal with. As we left the room, Luz said to him, "You will hear about us again and despite you and people like you we will make this product a success." I really loved her spirit.

The kids were still on my mind. Without the mortgage being paid on the family home, I worried about them losing the house and being left homeless. It made sense to me that the house should be sold, the debts paid and that whatever money was left could go towards a smaller but financially more practical house for them. A solicitor in Tipperary was representing me at this time and we decided to go there and discuss this with him. Against my solicitor's advice, I instructed him to inform my wife's solicitor that I would sign the house over to her so long as she agreed that all debts owing were paid from the proceeds of its sale. I didn't care if I got nothing out of it, so long as we could find some way to give the kids a home.

On leaving his office we went to the shopping centre. While there, Luz suggested that, since we were in Tipperary,

I should give the house a call and see if the kids could meet me. It was a long shot, but certainly worth a try. I called and my wife answered the phone. I told her I was at the shopping centre killing time before taking the train home and asked if I could see the kids. Her reply was, "They are not here and if they were they would not want to speak with you." And with that she hung up. I was disappointed that I would not see the children, but not at her answer; I had expected that.

Luz and I spent a little time browsing in the centre before leaving for our train. As we were walking out of the car park, we heard a car door being slammed shut. Looking in the direction of the sound, we saw my wife heading in our direction. She brushed straight past me, headed for Luz and started shouting at the top of her voice, "You foreign bitch, coming here and stealing my husband!"

It was outrageous behaviour and drew the attention of everyone in the car park. I really admired how Luz handled her. Remaining calm and dignified, she ignored the insult and linked my arm, saying, "Let's go home, honey." Luz had not taken the bait, as my wife had hoped, by lowering herself to the level of a shouting match in a public place. The irony of her accusing Luz of stealing something that she had happily thrown away was not lost on me. Although we did not rise to her bait, it was nonetheless another embarrassing moment caused by that woman. It now seemed that, as she had been prepared to drive to the car park just for the sake of verbally abusing us, then she would stop at nothing to interfere in our life, even if it meant making an exhibition of herself and us.

When we got to the train station, we had arrived a little early for the train, so we sat in the waiting-room and discussed what had happened. Sitting with Luz's hand in mine, I remembered the day when I had almost taken my life in this place. I went back to that moment in my mind but all I saw was another world and a man about to jump onto the tracks who was now a stranger to me. I had not died that day but he was well and truly buried. I was happy to have laid him to rest and in so doing reclaimed my sanity and my soul.

I was talking to Lorraine on the mobile as the announcement for the train to Dublin was made. I walked out of the waiting-room immersed in the conversation when a hard and sudden blow to the side of my face sent me reeling. For a moment I didn't know what was happening, but as my head cleared I thought I must be hallucinating. Standing in front of me were my wife and children. I found myself trying to cover up as best I could from the kicks and blows that rained down on me. It was the only way I could defend myself. I was certainly not going to strike out at my wife. Apart from my belief that nothing could justify a man striking a woman, I knew, even though I was dazed and shocked, how much damage she would try to cause me if I ever did, even if it was in self-defence. I had already been at the wrong end of false accusations in the past and I would never give a truth to those lies. Poor Luz also put herself in the way of the blows to try to protect me.

I could not believe this. She had rounded up my kids and obviously wound them up with some outrageous story about me and Luz. Now the children, who less than an hour earlier she had said were not in the house, had been deliberately brought to the station where I was attacked. (They had no other reason to be there.) I really wondered what sort of a mind could deliberately do that.

Luz and I finally managed to get ourselves out of the waiting-room area and onto the platform, but still she followed us, shouting her abusive and racist remarks at Luz, calling her a "foreign bitch" in front of the kids and all of the people on the platform. She was telling anyone who would listen that Luz had come here and stolen her husband. Luz had heard enough and shouted back at her, "Only an unfit mother would come here with her children and do such a thing to their father. What sort of conduct is that teaching them?" One of the station staff intervened and, thankfully, they went on their way and left us alone.

I was shocked and heartbroken by what had just happened. Although I did not blame my kids – I knew only too well how they were the innocents in all of this – it did nothing to ease the pain or the heartache. As the train approached, a thought entered my mind. This woman had now proven how far she would go to hurt me and Luz, and I would not put it past her to be in the police station now, accusing me and Luz of some wrongdoing. I knew only too well how her mind worked. I told Luz of my fears and that I thought it was important that we put what had happened on record in case she gave a false statement about these events.

And would you believe, as we entered the front door of Thurles Garda station, who do you think was sitting there, bold as brass, giving an Oscar-winning performance, telling the police that Luz and I had assaulted them? What made it worse was the reception we got when we entered the station; we were treated as if we were already guilty before they had even heard our side of the story. It was infuriating, but there was nothing that we could do but bite our tongues and wait our turn. When we did get our chance to speak, we pointed out that we were the ones that had been followed, first to the shopping centre and then to the train station, where we had been set upon and harassed. We had been deliberately sought out by her.

After they had taken our statements, we were asked to wait and after a few minutes they told us we were free to go – the kids had told them the truth of what had happened. We were asked if we were going to press charges and I replied, "What do you think?" It was only because she was the mother of my children that Luz and I decided not to press charges.

That whole episode was a horrible experience and I was embarrassed that Luz was being subjected to this abusive and outrageous behaviour. "That's what she wants, Noel. She thinks she is going to scare me off, but she is going to be one disappointed woman." We boarded the train and went home.

Needless to say, my mother and Lorraine were left speechless when we told them what had happened. Like us, they worried about the effects that all of this would have on the kids. Since the break-up of the marriage, it was not just me who had been denied access to my children. My mother, the children's grandmother, as well as Lorraine and all of my brothers and sisters – the children's aunts and uncles – and their children, my children's cousins, all were now deprived of any contact with my children. It was especially heartbreaking for my mother, who adores her grandchildren.

21

Tears and Fears

After the fiasco with the enterprise boards, we tried the banks – and by banks, I mean practically every bank in Dublin – to see if we could secure the finance to manufacture the product. The response was always the same: "No!" They either thought that we were ridiculous thinking of making money from a product that used paper waste or they would ask us if we had security to cover a loan. Security! If we had the damn security, we would not need the loan. It was so frustrating, having put so much hard work into our product and business plan, only to find that no one was willing to take a chance on us when it came to providing the all-important finance.

Things were further complicated because Luz's application for a business permission was still under review. She only had leave to stay in the country on a temporary basis until the decision was made. At this moment, that decision could go either way. Vital to us securing that permission was being able to prove that we had a viable business, capable of providing for Luz's needs if she were given permission to stay. The Department of Justice were being as helpful and understanding as they could, but if we did not secure the finance to fund the business and ourselves, then Luz would be asked to leave the country.

I can remember so well both of us sitting dejected on the ground of the first floor of Stephen's Green Shopping Centre, next to a radio broadcasting booth located there. We had just come from another bank that had give us another resounding "No". With only a month left on Luz's extension to her visa, it seemed inevitable that she would be heading back to the Philippines. The thought that we could be separated, torn apart after all that we had overcome together, was too much to take. Sitting there looking at Luz's passport with the stamp indicating the date of expiration for her visa, we both succumbed to the pressure we were under. Sitting on the floor, we hugged each other and gave way to our emotions as the tears filled our eyes.

I have never been a member of a political party or had a particular affiliation with any political party, but Luz and I will always be indebted to Gay Mitchell MEP for the outstanding work he did on our behalf with regard to Luz's business permission application. With nowhere else to turn and time running out, we visited Gay at his constituency offices, not far from my mother's house in Walkinstown, and told him of our dilemma. Gay was genuinely impressed by our product and immediately latched on to its positive environmental qualities. Through his efforts, the efforts of his wife Norma and his aide John Staunton, the representations that they made to the Department of Justice on Luz's behalf managed to secure an extension on her visa while her business permission was still under review. It was only a temporary reprieve but at least it gave us some breathing space and time to keep looking for that all-important finance.

Having been to watch a movie in Liffey Valley Shopping Centre in an effort to chill out for a couple of hours, we sat on a bench in the mall and browsed the evening newspaper. For no particular reason, I browsed the property page and an advertisement for a house to rent in Lucan caught my eye. There were a lot of houses listed for rent; why that particular one took my notice I cannot tell you, but out of a spirit of optimism, I said to Luz, "Let's call this number and have a look at that house."

Luz looked at me, puzzled. "Are you mad, honey? We had to scrape together the money to watch this movie today – how on earth do you think we can afford to rent a house?"

I knew she was right but I needed to be positive. In the end I convinced Luz to go along with me. What else had we to do?

When we arrived for the viewing of the house, there were several other people there, all of them extremely interested in it. Maybe Luz had been right; it was a little depressing reminding myself of what I could not have. We were walking out the front door when the agent called to me and handed me her card, "If you are interested, call this number at GPK Properties and we will be delighted to talk to you." GPK . . . that name was familiar to me.

"Is that Gerry Kinsella's company?" I asked, wondering if it was the same Gerry Kinsella I had sold and bought houses from in the past. She confirmed that it was. After she took my phone number, Luz and I went on our way.

The following day I received a phone call from Gerry. He had recognised my name. After a brief chat, he invited me to call into his offices and we set a date to meet later in the week.

Sitting in Gerry's office, Luz was a little embarrassed at taking up this man's time when we had no money to rent a property from him. Gerry obviously wondered why I was with Luz now and not my wife – so we told him our story. As I neared the end of the tale, Gerry stood looking out the window. When I finished, he turned around and I could see in his eyes that he was genuinely saddened over what had happened to us. Unbelievably, he then handed us the keys to the house, saying, "Move into that house tomorrow."

"But, Gerry, we don't have the money to pay for that house. Thanks all the same." I was thankful that he would have given us first choice to take it.

"Noel, I didn't ask if you could afford to pay for it – just move into it and I will work out something," he said, smiling. Luz and I looked at him in disbelief.

But Gerry meant every word. Before the week was over, we had moved into a brand new fully furnished house. It was like a dream.

Gerry then met with Luz and me again and he asked us about the product and what we were trying to do with it. When we had finished explaining our product to Gerry, he told us that his daughter was a researcher on RTÉ's *Open House* TV show. He would try to organise for us to appear on the show. It would be a good opportunity to look for investors in the product.

True to Gerry's word, we appeared on the show hosted by Mary Kennedy and Marty Whelan. It gave us the opportunity to showcase the product and appeal for investors to move it forward. We also used this opportunity to thank all of the people who were already supporting us in one way or another. These included Steve Lennon from Hasbro, Gay Mitchell, Colum Foley from Eason's, and Luz's Credit Union who, after many meetings, had given approval to Luz for a loan of € 30,000 for the business. This approval from the credit union was a great boost for the business permission application, because it would show that we had funds in the business account.

We followed up this TV appearance with another one on TV3's *Ireland AM* show, which offered us another welcome opportunity to showcase the product and solicit investors. It was exciting and a little hard to believe that, within a few weeks, we had gone from sleeping on a floor to living in a fully furnished house and appearing on national television. We still had no money but things were moving in the right direction.

About a week after appearing on the TV show, we started doing follow-up calls to all of the people we had mentioned, just to keep in touch and let them know that we were still actively pushing forward with our plans for the product. But something was wrong. Everyone I spoke to seemed to be responding to me very differently than before. The conversations were colder than usual. At first,

I put it down to me just being over-anxious and sensitive, but when the credit union withdrew the loan offer, we knew something serious was wrong.

I could not understand what was happening; but Luz could. "I bet you anything, honey, that your wife has been in touch with everyone we mentioned on that TV show and attempted to bad-mouth you or both of us to them."

Luz was right. I called Steve Lennon and Colum Foley and they both confirmed that my wife had called them and more or less warned them off doing business with me. Both Colum and Steve said that their coolness to me was not an indication of judgement of me but more a case of not wanting to get caught in the middle of a family dispute. Having spoken to both of them, I will always be grateful for how, on reflection, they both said to me that they had never seen anything wrong with me and that, at the end of the day, there are two sides to every story. They had obviously questioned her motives for calling them and involving them in our personal life. Luz and I had salvaged our relationship with these people and, on a personal level much more than on a business one, I was relieved.

The outcome was not so satisfactory, however, with the credit union. At first they would not take our calls. When they did, their replies as to why they had withdrawn the loan offer to Luz were very cryptic. It was only after pressing the matter further that they admitted they had received a phone call from my wife. What really upset us about this was the fact that it was Luz and not I who was the credit union member. It was now clear to us that Luz was being penalised by her association with me and on the hearsay of a vindictive phone call. Luz did consider filing a case against my wife and the credit union because of this and how it reflected on her character. But she decided not to pursue it, only because of how it might have been used by my wife to further turn my kids against me.

My scheming wife's attack on us was completed when a summons for a maintenance order was served on me. She obviously thought that I had money because I was on TV and talking about our product. Nothing motivated that woman more than money. So despite the fact that I was surviving on a disability payment from social welfare and only had a roof over my head thanks to the generosity first of my family and then of Gerry, I found myself once again before Thurles District Court for no good reason.

When called by the court to give my evidence, I explained my circumstances and went on to say that since the day my children were born I had provided for them, even putting myself into debt to keep all of them happy and that, with all due respect, I did not need any court to remind me of my obligations as a father. I went on to explain that, by appearing on national television, broadcasting to everyone what I was trying to do, I was being as open as humanly possible about my financial status. These were not the actions of a man trying to hide anything. I finished by saying that my motivation for succeeding in this business was not just for personal gain – I wanted to be in a position where I could provide for my children. I asked the question, "Why would any mother try to bad-mouth the father of her children to the people he was trying to do business with in his open and transparent efforts to put himself in a position to provide for her children?" But I knew the answer. It was because she would rather see me suffer for her own selfish reasons than see me succeed and in so doing benefit the kids. What else could have been achieved by her malicious phone calls, had they succeeded, other than my complete and utter ruin and the dragging down of Luz alongside me?

I had been honest in my evidence, which is more than can be said for her. When questioned by her solicitor in the court, she had given evidence that she was just surviving on a social welfare payment and that this was her only source of income. But when cross-questioned and faced with information that my solicitor had gathered, she had to admit that she had turned what used to be my office in the house into a hair salon, that she was earning money from it and that she was also working in FÁS doing hairdressing instruction. When my solicitor asked why she had not mentioned this when asked previously, she brazenly answered, "I forgot."

The judge dismissed her claim, saying that he was satisfied that I did not have money and he was assured that if I did I would continue to care for my kids. It was another victory, but once again a hollow one. Perhaps she had told my kids that their father was on TV and that he had lots of money but that he did not want to give them any. I am also sure she told them that she was going to have to take him to court to force him to support them, because that is what she did. But I considered from previous experience that they would never hear from her the truth of the matter or the ruling made by the judge.

I have a huge amount of respect for women and perhaps this is because of my upbringing and the fact that I have three sisters and worked for twenty years of my life with women. But it really frustrated me to discover day-by-day how much the system is weighted in favour of the woman and just how easy it is for a small number of manipulative women to abuse that system for their own needs.

Take what was happening to me as an example. My wife could lay accusation after accusation at my feet as the fancy took her. Even though they were without foundation, I still had to go to court, incurring unnecessary expenses to defend myself against them. This cannot be right. I have never been charged with any type of offence whatsoever in my life, and yet I had to defend a barring order under the Domestic Violence Act. Why? But more worryingly, imagine how my future life would have been marred had such an order been granted against me.

I was only receiving a disability payment and yet I was brought to court to defend an application made against me for a maintenance order. Why? I was unable to work because I was dealing with a mental problem caused by severe depression, but even so I was doing everything possible to improve my life. What was her excuse? She was not disabled. She did not have young babies to care for and we were living in a booming economy with any number of jobs on offer. She was also a qualified hairdresser. What was to stop her earning a living?

The family home – our family home – had one of its rooms converted without any notification to me. The locks on our family home had been changed without any notification to me. But worse than the changing of the locks was the message which that action was sending out to my children and the neighbours. I could not get access to personal possessions and even when I only requested pictures of the kids, pictures of me as a child and pictures of my deceased father, I was told through her solicitor and on her instructions, "No."

But for me the proof of the inequality in the system was proved by what she did next. Luz and I decided to take a trip to Tipperary after we had received news that my wife and kids were no longer living in the house there. Sure enough, when we arrived at the house it was vacated – and she had stripped it. She had emptied a 3,500-square-foot house of every possession – not her possessions, *our possessions*. My tools, clothes, my personal belongings and memories I had accumulated over twenty years, were all gone.

My daughter who was still a minor at the time, had been removed by my wife from the family home without any notification to me, her father, as to where she was now residing. I had obeyed every rule of the law – now here she was, totally disrespecting it and me. If this was equality, if this showed how you would be made to suffer when you tried to live your life as a good man, flawed though some of your decisions might have been, I could not begin to imagine what was suffered by those who deserved it.

But the frustration and anger I was feeling over the abuses to the system and to me were to pale into insignificance compared to the sadness I was about to encounter.

I had not seen my daughter or son in more than two years. Since their mother had moved them from the family home, I did not even have the peace of mind of knowing where they were living. Luz and I were driving through Lucan village one afternoon when Luz jumped up suddenly in her seat. Pointing as we turned a corner, she said excitedly, "Look, Noel, there's your daughter." I slowed the car and my heart leapt for joy when I saw my daughter walking with a group of school kids. She had grown so much since I had last seen her. She was wearing a uniform I recognised as being from a girl's school in Lucan.

I was conscious of the fact that, if I suddenly stopped the car and called out to my daughter, I might startle and upset her. It saddened me to think that I had to consider how I was going to approach my daughter, my own flesh and blood, but I had been demonised in her eyes and I could not predict the reaction I would get. I drove about 150 yards past her to a part of the road that was safe and got out of the car, waiting for her to pass my way. I was going to see my little girl at last. Even though she was now sixteen she was still my little girl and I missed her so much.

As my daughter came into view, I was amazed at how she had grown; she was a young woman. I felt a lump in my throat as I thought about the lost years since I had last seen her. I called out her name, walking towards her and holding my hands out in welcome as she caught sight of me. I was smiling but my heart was pounding. Soon I would be holding my daughter, my little girl, in my arms again.

But when she saw me, she looked at me as if I was a stranger, quickening her pace as she side-stepped me and walked straight past me. My heart sank. I could smell her, see her, but I could not touch her. Every instinct in my body wanted to run after her, hold her and tell her how much I loved her and missed her, but I knew I couldn't do that. I knew that if my daughter did not voluntarily come to me, then her mother would have a field day with the police if I put a hand on her, even if that hand held all of my love. So I stood there and watched her go by. The little girl I had put to bed every night since she was born; the little girl who told me she was going to marry me when she grew up; the little girl who owned a huge part of my heart, walked away from me as if I was a stranger.

I stood there by the side of the road looking after her and trying to keep my composure, unable to accept what had just happened. Luz, who had stayed in the car and witnessed what had happened, called me over to her. "I know, Noel," she said, seeing the distress in my face as I got back into the car. I did not reply to Luz. I couldn't. I was choked and barely holding myself together. I swung the car around and as I passed by my daughter I let down the window and shouted across the road to her, "I love you." I knew she heard me but she did not acknowledge me.

I continued to drive until I found a quiet road and parked the car. I put my head on the steering wheel and cried. I cried and cried until I couldn't cry any more as my heart, which had already been broken, was pulverised and smashed into a million pieces. Luz did her best to try to console me, telling me it wasn't my daughter's fault and that one day she would know a different truth. But the only truth I could see was that my little girl was gone.

When I had composed myself, I started the car, gave Luz a kiss and drove back home.

The only good thing to come out of this was that at least I knew where my daughter was going to school. I could enquire there about her welfare and how she was doing in that school. It should have been straightforward – I was her father, she was my daughter and I was entitled to meet with her teachers and see how she was progressing. But it was not like that. I could have just walked into the school unannounced and asked to speak to someone but if my presence there was going to upset my daughter and distract her from her studies, I was not going to do that. So I rang to make an appointment and to try to arrange my meeting in a way that would be in my daughter's best interests. I lost count of the number of phone calls that I made and the unanswered messages that I left. When I finally got to speak with the principal I was told she would have to speak to the board of management before she could give me an appointment to discuss my daughter's schooling.

I could not believe this. I was not a criminal, I was a separated man whose marriage had failed, and yet I was being treated as if I was some sort of low-life. I wondered what lies had been told about me this time. No explanation can do justice to the feelings of hurt and frustration that come from being judged and found guilty by people who don't know you and who know nothing whatsoever about you or your life. They base their opinion of you on whatever they have heard through malicious lies and gossip and never consider that there might be another side to the story.

In the end I had to hire a solicitor to write to the school and point out to them my rights and entitlements to know about my daughter's education and welfare in that school. When I was still living with my kids' mother, I attended every single school meeting or event that required my presence. I helped in any way that I could in any events in which the children were involved. But now, just because I was separated, I had to hire a solicitor to talk to a teacher. What made it worse was that my daughter had attended the primary part of the same school and all that I was telling them in the secondary school could easily be verified.

Eventually I got my meeting but it was wrong what they had put me through to get it. I fully respected that they had to put the welfare of the child first, but a quick check through any police station would have shown them that I had no criminal record of any nature and therefore posed no threat to my daughter.

I'd had enough. I needed to bring closure to this episode in my life. If I was ever to have the freedom to move forward into the future without the threat of my wife's hands all the time reaching out and trying to strangle my efforts to improve my life, I would need proper legal representation. I needed someone in my corner who could look after all of this family law stuff, not just to defend me against scurrilous attacks but to set in motion whatever was required to end my marriage to that woman.

But legal representation requires money and I had none. I went to the citizen's advice centre and asked about free legal aid. It was available to me, but the waiting list was huge. Luz and I were already more than motivated to succeed in our life, but knowing that the success of our products would provide the finance for my legal needs gave extra impetus to our efforts and made us even more determined to succeed. Thankfully, through Gerry's intervention, we would soon take a giant leap towards that dream.

22

Highs and Lows

Gerry Kinsella was also appalled by what was happening and how it was impacting on Luz and me. One day while meeting with him in his office, Gerry said that he wanted to introduce us to a very good friend of his called Dónall Curtin, a partner in the firm Byrne Curtin Kelly Accountants. Gerry thought that Dónall, who was passionate about art and the environment, would be very interested in our product. Gerry set up the meeting with Dónall. So, armed with our samples and the very same business plan we had submitted to everyone else, we walked into Dónall's office.

We were no more than ten minutes into our presentation when Dónall told us to stop. Luz and I of course thought that we were going to receive the same comments that we had received from all the other financial institutions to date. But we were wrong. Dónall loved the product and following that meeting we set in motion the plans to form a company to exploit it. Dónall and Gerry agreed to finance the project and would provide us with a salary once the paperwork was complete. In return, Dónall and Gerry received shares in that company, which now owned the product. Luz and I were delighted. It was the breakthrough that we had been waiting for and it also secured Luz's business permission.

Just days before this meeting, we had been in the house and had run out of milk. We had no money except what was in a jar of spare cents that Luz had been saving. She checked and confirmed that we had enough to buy a litre of milk. So into the shop we walked, picked up the milk and handed the coins to the shop assistant. As we prepared to walk away, we heard the coins falling onto the counter as the assistant said, "Just a moment! Can you count these? How am I supposed to know how much is here?" So, one by one, we counted each cent to him as the other customers looked on. It was humiliating. Hopefully those days were now behind us.

We formed the company and, at my suggestion, called it "Luz Java Ltd". There were two reasons for this. Firstly, because we were dealing in the toy industry, I wanted our company to be seen as being made up of real hands-on people – that Luz Java was a real person with integrity and that she represented the honesty and commitment behind our products and what those products promised to deliver in terms of playability. Secondly, so many people in Luz's life had underestimated her and taken her for granted; maybe now, when they saw our company name, they would not underestimate her again.

With Dónall and Gerry, we drew up a plan of action for progressing the product. Having decided that we were going down the road of self-manufacturing, we set our sights on being able to showcase the product to the trade at the UK Toy Fair, scheduled for January 2005. We would also have to file any new patents and trademarks that were required and source product designers who could bring the product to manufacturing standard. We also had to book and organise our stand for the toy fair as well as source graphic designers to work on our logos. There was a lot to do and the clock had already started ticking.

Our brief to the product designers was very precise. It had to be; it was June 2004 and with the staging of the 2005 UK Toy Fair only seven months away, it left little time for us to prepare for the exhibition. Buyers from all over the world would be present, making this fair one of the most important in the toy industry's calendar and a "must attend" event for anyone hoping to secure orders for the forthcoming year. A mammoth task lay ahead if we were to meet the deadline for exhibiting at the fair. Display stands would have to be designed and built; the work on the logos for the products and our company would need to be completed and trademarked; there would certainly be further patents to be applied for, not to mention the huge variety of samples to be made showing the output from the craft kit; but such was our hunger for success that none of this phased us.

Our fate would rest in the hands of the product designers we had chosen. Success or failure would hinge on their delivering of the design brief on time. It was crucial that the designs and prototype they produced would be representative of a toy and so we made it crystal clear that the finished product should look "fun" and entice the consumer to "play with it". Happy in the knowledge that we had clearly and concisely conveyed our instructions, we began to work on addressing some of the weaknesses in our company.

Of course, there were lots of strengths in our company. However, the problem remained that none of us possessed "hands-on" experience of the intricacies of the toy business. We addressed this problem by hiring an expert named Tim Garner. Tim had worked for Tiger Electronics and was the man responsible for launching "Furby", a global phenomenon in the toy world. Furby, an electronic plush toy, topped many top ten lists across the world when it was first released in 1998 and since then in excess of forty million Furby creatures had been sold worldwide.

When the designs arrived, Luz and I spent the entire weekend appraising them. As we sat on our living-room floor, far removed from the high-tech virtual world of the design studio, computer-aided drawings and specifications strewn about us, our blood ran cold as the terrible truth was revealed. Mechanically, what the designers had proposed could not work. Added to this, they had introduced batteries. Introducing batteries into a toy that was promoting an environmental message made no sense. There was also a real commercial concern that introducing motors and electronics would make it impossible for us to manufacture the product for a price that was competitive. To top it all, our product now looked more like a fax machine than a plaything. It was a disaster and it sent our heads spinning.

The day that we had scheduled to meet with the designers and Steve Lennon in order to discuss our concerns over the designs was also the day that we met Tim Garner for the very first time. We met with Tim in Dónall's office a few hours prior to the meeting with the designers. When Tim saw our products, which included a new stacking game called Tumba, he was totally blown away by them. However, when we showed Tim the designs put forward by the design company, he shared our surprise and disappointment, saying, "They have *got* to be joking."

And so, later that day, Tim, Steve Lennon, Luz and I sat to one side of the boardroom table as we waited for the designers to join us in their studio. The atmosphere was tense. There was a very real threat that our plans to launch the product at the 2005 UK Toy Fair were going to be shattered. Luz was feeling every bit as disappointed as I was, but somehow she managed to remain calm. It was a trait I envied in her. No matter how daunting the situation facing her, she managed to retain her composure and take it in her stride. Perhaps that was why we were such a good team. We often joked that we were like "fire and ice", and I suppose we had learned to balance the opposites. We knew each other so well that, without even saying a word, I could see in Luz's eyes that she was telling me to calm down; she was controlling my fire.

The product designers finally joined us in their meeting-room and I introduced them to Steve and Tim, forcing a smile through gritted teeth as I waited for the pleasantries to end. "Now, gentlemen," I said, fixing both designers with my stare, "these designs are just not good enough!" Luz and I went on to explain our grievances to them, followed by Tim and Steve giving their professional critique of the design, which totally validated our concerns. To our amazement, the designers defended their flawed designs for the mechanism by trying to tell us that all that was need was a change of colour scheme.

Had we not already been into these guys for a considerable amount of money – over €30,000 to be precise – Luz and I would have been happy to walk away from them. But I'd heard enough of their nonsense and so, without saying a word, I began to sketch an exploded view of the proposed mechanism, exposing the unsound principles in its design and proving the fact that it could not possibly function as proposed. My tactic worked. After an embarrassing silence, they finally acknowledged the flawed design. The meeting ended with the designers undertaking to revisit their design and Luz and I reiterating to them the urgency of the timeframe involved.

We were also awaiting work from graphic designers at this time. We had commissioned and briefed them for the work to be done on our company logo and the logos for our products. It had been a week since the fiasco with the product designers but, with the memory of it fresh in our minds, we were more than a little apprehensive about how they had handled that brief. Unfortunately for Luz and I, our apprehension had been well-founded. We were presented with graphics that, at the very best, could only be described as being convoluted and strained. The graphics were so wide of the mark that we did not even bother to argue our case with them – we just left.

This was not a happy time for us as day by day we found ourselves going backwards while time raced on at a frightening pace. Our dream was now hanging on a thread.

Next day, Luz looked tired as we waited in the product designers' office. We had both slept very little over the last few weeks, pushing ourselves both mentally and physically, consumed by the worry of what the product designers were going to present us with.

We were right to be worried. Luz and I just stared in total disbelief at what they presented to us. They had done absolutely nothing! The styling of the product looked exactly the same and, although they had removed the need for batteries, the device still contained the same flawed mechanism as before. It was a bad dream; it had to be. This could not be happening. *These are professional designers and professional designers don't do things like this*, I thought to myself, hoping that I would soon wake up from the nightmare.

Luz and I were furious. There was absolutely no way that we could now make the deadline for exhibiting at the fair. Years of hard work, our hopes for success and our dream for a better life, seemed shattered. So many thoughts were going through our heads. How would our investors react to this news? How could we explain that, after spending their money on patents, designers, logos and a consultant, we did not have a product to exhibit? And how would they react when they heard that it would be another full year before the opportunity to exhibit came again?

23

Homecoming Dream

Luz and I had been dreading the meeting with Dónall and Gerry; they had put so much faith in us. Thankfully, our fears were unfounded. They fully acknowledged the hard work that Luz and I were putting into everything and firmly lay the blame at the feet of the product and graphic designers. Gerry and Dónall advised us to put the disappointment behind us and not to worry; they would back us all the way to get our products to the market. We had always said that we had found "angels" and not investors when we found Dónall and Gerry, and now we knew just how true that statement was. It was such a relief to know that we had another chance to get it right and could now focus all of our attention on the 2006 Toy Fair.

Over the course of the next few weeks, Dónall, Gerry, Luz and I met with the product designers in an effort to try to find a way to move forward with them, but it became increasingly clear that the only way forward would be to cut our ties with them and look elsewhere. We decided to mark down our dealings with them to experience, move on and find a design house who *could* give us what we wanted. It did, however, raise a dilemma – for, God help us, the designers we had been using were supposedly the best in the country. Where on earth did we go from here?

Luz and I flopped down onto the sofa, more than a little exhausted by the day's events. Being physically tired was one thing – at least a good night's sleep would sort that out – but being mentally tired was something totally different. Our brains were totally preoccupied with sourcing new designers who would fully understand our objectives. I was really beginning to hate the word "designers". Luz switched on the TV. The programme that was showing was called *The Apprentice*, a reality TV show where two teams are given challenges relating to the business world. The main focus of the show is businessman Alan Sugar. Luz and I had not seen the programme before, but within seconds of Alan Sugar describing that week's challenge, we were riveted to the screen. "Now teams," he said, "your challenge for this week is to design a toy. Each team will be given a design company to work with and the team to design the best toy, as judged by one of the leading toy companies in Europe, will win the challenge." Luz and I could not believe our ears. Had Alan Sugar just given us the answer to our design problem?

As soon as the programme was finished, Luz and I bombarded the BBC with phone calls in an attempt to make contact with the production company behind the programme. A few days later, our persistence paid off. We spoke to the producers of the programme and they provided us with the contact details of the design company featured on the show. They were called "designworks" and they were based in Windsor. A few days later, with bags packed and tickets in hand, we set off for Dublin Airport.

Our taxi turned into Windsor Business Centre and came to a stop outside the offices of designworks. We were excited at the prospect of meeting these designers and eager to get the project back on track. The moment we entered their offices we knew that we had made the right decision. There was a vitality and dynamism about the place. The reception area was decorated with samples of projects that the company had worked on and it was an impressive variety of work, but more importantly for Luz and I, there were lots of toy designs. The owners of the company, Jeremy and Pete, greeted us and took us to their meeting-room where they introduced us to Andrea, one of their senior designers. There followed an in-depth and detailed discussion where the entire design brief and the way forward was fully discussed.

Dealing with these people was like a breath of fresh air. They fully understood our objectives and spent so much time to ensure that our thought processes were the same; even at this early stage their input was impressive. Luz and I were smiling again and it felt very, very good.

Luz

It had been years since Noel or I had taken a holiday and so with all of our work up to date and the work on the prototype safely in the hands of designworks, we booked our tickets and flew to the Philippines. I had not seen my family in almost five years and the excitement of knowing that I would soon be seeing them all again – added to the fact that I would at last see my Richard for the first time in sixteen years – made this homecoming very, very special for me.

It was so fitting that Noel should be with me on this trip, for without him none of this would have been possible. I was so proud to be introducing Noel to my family, to show them the man who had changed my life and who had given me more love than I ever knew existed. Noel was like a child as we touched down at Davao airport. At last he would see my country and he was excited and curious to see all of the places I had told him about in my story. When I had left the Philippines all those years ago, disillusioned, hurt and betrayed, I never dared dream that I would return like this with the man that I loved on my arm and my long-lost son waiting to greet me with the rest of my children.

Everything was arranged for us when we stepped out of the airport. There was a van waiting to collect us with what can only be described as a battalion of excited people prepared and ready to take our luggage and bring us to my sister Fern's house. When we pulled into the street and stopped outside Fern's house, there was a big banner across the front of the door saying "Welcome Noel and Luz" and my mother, my sister Fern and my sister-in-law Adela were there to greet us and welcome us into the house.

Immediately I was hugged and kissed by Charmie and Charlon, and I could not believe how much they had grown since I had last seen them. The tears flowed and I thought my heart would burst with pride and happiness when I saw Noel embrace my children. In that moment we became the family I had always wanted. Noel had always said that my children were now his children and that he would love them as if they were his very own. Now I could see that my children were at last going to have the father that they never knew or had. It all seemed so natural, so easy, as if we had always been a family, and Noel blended in as if he had lived there all of his life. Herlene and Hermson, who were still in Polomolok living with Hermie's mother, would be travelling to see us the following day.

The house had been full of noise with the excitement of my homecoming, when suddenly it went very quiet. A young man had entered the room and as he stood by the door I knew it was my Richard. I ran to him and in the time it took me to cover the couple of metres between us, I relived every moment of the pain of losing my baby. I remembered his little baby face wrapped in his baby blanket as I kissed him goodbye and handed him to Emily – the last kiss I had ever given him. I wrapped my arms around him. No words were needed and none were spoken. Together at last, we felt each other's pain and experienced each other's joy while the torrent of our uncontrollable tears spoke all the words we needed to say. When I finally managed to let Richard go, with a lump in my throat I just about managed to say, "I love you, son, and you will always be my baby."

Noel came over to join us and with tears in his eyes, he hugged us both tightly to him. I cannot really describe what that meant to me. At last I had a man who would never deny my children and I thanked God for the miracle of Noel and the miracle of this day.

When we finally managed to compose ourselves, we sat at the large table, which was so crammed full of food that you could not see the surface of the table below it, and we ate with the rest of the family. During the meal, Noel turned to me and said, "I know, sweetheart, that you never gave up hope of finding your son. What I just witnessed, watching you both reunited, was a wonderful thing to behold and something I will remember for the rest of my life."

"But, honey, you weren't just a witness. You were the most important part in all of this. I found Richard but, without your love and understanding, Richard would never have found me!" I don't think I have ever felt so in love as I did in that moment.

When things settled down, we sat and talked. I was so proud to introduce Noel to everyone. He told me that he instantly felt at home in this place and with the people. Noel said it was not just the weather that was warm, it was the people too. He joked that it was very reminiscent of how we entertain in Ireland at family gatherings. He would soon learn that Filipinos were also like the Irish when it came to singing, just needing the slightest bit of encouragement to sing a song or take to the stage.

The following day, Noel and I were joined by Herlene and Hermson. As we sat in our hotel room, I experienced for the very first time in my life all five of my children together. It was the stuff of dreams and it was made even more special when we were joined by Charmie's son Ian, my grandson. For the very first time in my life, I felt complete.

We spent that holiday as one big happy family, enjoying the sights and being with each other. My mother joined us as we toured Davao. Although we were glad to see each other, there would never be a closeness between us; it was just not in her nature and I had accepted that. All the closeness that I needed I now had with Noel and my kids, and back in Ireland I had a family who loved me. What more could I wish for?

When it was time for the kids to go home, I asked Richard to stay back a while with me so that I could talk to him. We both knew there were so many questions to answer and, hard as it would be to revisit the past, we needed to understand why his abduction had happened and I needed to let him know that I never gave up on him. I had feared that, when Richard and I finally met, the distance the years had put between us would be too big a void to bridge and that he would be unable to see or accept me as his mother. But my fears were unfounded. There was an intangible bond between us and we both knew where we really belonged, and that was with each other.

I asked him how he was feeling about everything that had happened and if there was anything he needed to know or ask me. Richard told me that he had been so confused by everything that had happened and that he was still trying to adjust to this tumultuous change in his life. He was happy to know the truth of his birth and to know me and his brothers and sisters, even if this new knowledge was challenging everything that he had believed himself to be. He felt that he was being torn in two. One half of him was filled with love for the people whom he had believed were his parents and the other half of him was filled with anger for the lie that he had been allowed to live.

I tried to push him for information on the people that Emily had given him to but all that I got out of him was that they were the parents of Emily's husband and that they had changed his birth certificate and his name into their family name. I could see that Richard was getting distraught at the questions and I knew he was struggling against his feelings of loyalty to these people by talking about them to me. I had to accept for the moment that I was the *stranger* in this situation and that it would take a long time for Richard and me to build a trust. It would serve no purpose to burden him with more than he could handle. What he needed now was space and I would have to be patient and wait for Richard to start asking his own questions.

The change in Richard's birth certificate had legal implications that needed to be sorted out and that could only be done by an attorney. Noel and I paid a visit to one of the leading legal practices in Davao and asked them their advice on all of this. After much discussion, it was clear that we could take a case against Emily and the parents of her husband, but to do so could be very damaging for Richard and ultimately to any future relationship with me. We asked Richard to accompany us to the meeting with the attorney and asked him what he wanted us to do. He told me that, if we continued with the case against his abductors, I would never see him again. Of course, it was painful to hear this, but I had to understand that he would be put in the position of giving evidence against the people he thought were his parents for the last sixteen years of his life and that evidence would send them to prison.

This posed a dilemma for me. I had waited for this moment for so long – the moment when I would finally get justice for the pain and heartache caused to me by Emily and her in-laws. But in receiving that justice, I could destroy the very thing I had craved and missed for so long – my son. My baby was not my baby any longer and I had to learn to love the man he had become, even if that man loved and had been fashioned by my tormentors. Richard was alive and that was what really mattered. I would have to try to let go of the past and be happy that we had a future.

Noel

For all of its history and troubled past, there was an innocence about this place and about the people who lived here. When Luz and I had sat on the sofa opening our suitcases, with all the kids and adults gathered around to see what goodies we might have brought them, it reminded me so much of the excitement I used to feel as a child when my aunt came home from America or my father came home after being on a trip to the UK. It really was like going back about thirty or forty years in time – and I say that as a compliment of the highest order. Community was important here, as it once used to be in Ireland, and the respect that the children had, not only for their parents but for other adults, made me yearn to be back in the days when this was also commonplace in my own country. I wondered if it was a mathematical equation or a universal law that seemed to dictate that, as the level of affluence increased in a country, the level of civility within its population seemed to decrease by the same degree.

Here among her own people, I got to see the real Luz and it was so obvious how much she loved and missed this place. The exuberance of the people, especially the teenagers and children, who had very little in terms of possessions when compared to their western counterparts, was inspiring. But despite having some beautiful places, with names to match such as Paradise Island or Eden Garden, this was no promised land. There was still a lot to be desired with regard to the welfare of the disadvantaged and the care of the infirm, but if paradise auditioned for inhabitants, it would be populated with Filipinos.

Victoria Plaza, located in J.P. Laurel Avenue, Bajada, is one of several very large shopping centres in Davao City. One day as we sat eating in Greenwich Pizza fast food restaurant with all of the kids, Luz turned to me and said, "Never in my wildest dreams, Noel, did I ever think that I would be sitting in a restaurant in Davao City surrounded by all five of my children and with the man that I love in the middle of us, one of us, and just loving us for who we are." I could see how much this meant to Luz. Finally, she was complete, with the love and the family that she had always craved now hers, to hold and to cherish. It was real and no longer a dream. "And imagine, Noel, I had to fly halfway around the world to touch a book that would find me the man who could make all of this happen for me. I love you so much." Luz then kissed my lips, much to the amusement and delight of her kids. I looked at all of the happy contented faces around me and I knew I had got the best part of this deal.

The holiday did us a power of good and was just the tonic we needed to set us up for the challenge that lay ahead. With much reluctance and lots of beautiful memories, we waved Davao and the Philippines goodbye and set our sights on home and making more dreams come true.

24

Little Miracles

Over the course of the next few months we worked hand-in-hand with designworks as we refined the prototype and improved on the process involved with its operation. By the time we had finished, we had produced a prototype and representation of our product of which we were proud and confident to offer to the consumer. There is a very talented and creative team of people working in designworks and such was our confidence in them that we also asked them to tackle our logos for us. We needed logos for our craft kit, which we had called "Paper FX", our stacking game called "Tumba", and for our Luz Java Ltd logo.

While designworks worked on the logos, we met up with our consultant, Tim Garner, and discussed with him the options available to us for distribution of our products and the organising of the exhibition space we required for the Toy Fair. Tim told us that he would look after whatever was required regarding the Toy Fair, as he had years of experience in this department. That left us to discuss how we would distribute our products once they were manufactured. Tim drew up a list of potential distributors in the UK and arranged meetings with them that the three of us – Tim, Luz and I – would attend.

The day that we spent attending those meetings was quite extraordinary. We went to meet these companies, who were significant players within the toy industry, merely to discuss distribution, but every single one of them responded by saying how fantastic they thought the products were and that they were more interested in acquiring the rights to them than simply distributing them. It was amazing, because it is notoriously difficult to successfully license new products to manufacturers within the toy and games industry. There was something ironic in the fact that, in the early days of the product, we had been unsuccessful in trying to license it, but now, because we had decided to manufacture it ourselves, we were being asked to license it!

But the most amusing and ironic moment of the day was kept for our last meeting. When the company personnel saw our products, they loved them and, like the other companies that we had visited that day, they also wanted to secure worldwide licensing rights to them. The irony was that the name of this company was Flair Leisure Products plc – the very company that had declined the product when Steve Lennon had shown it to them previously on our behalf. Yes, the product had come a long way since they had first seen it, but if ever proof were needed that you should never take "no" for an answer, then this was certainly it.

The following weeks were spent weighing up all of the options available to us. Now that the option to license the products was available, we made the decision to go that route. It gave us the best opportunity of exploiting the product globally within the shortest period of time. All that remained for us to decide was to which company we would license the rights for our products. It came down to two companies. Both were UK-based and offered different reasons as to why we should choose them. One of them was among the largest toy companies in the UK; they had huge resources behind them and could throw a lot of weight behind the product. The downside was that they did not wish to develop our products as brands in their own right; they wanted to absorb them into an existing brand that they controlled. The other company was Flair. They were a smaller company but appeared to have a wealth of experience in the toy business. More importantly for us, they shared our view of building Paper FX into a brand. We were extremely flattered that the bigger of these two companies was interested in our product and appreciated the time they had given us, but the fact that Flair were interested in developing the Paper FX brand swung it in their favour. So we agreed to do the deal with them.

The contracts needed to be drawn up and through the Golden Pages we sourced a firm of solicitors called Amory's in Sandyford, Dublin. It was another crazy, serendipitous moment in our lives. We met with Sharon Scally, a delightful woman and the owner of the firm. Luz and I explained to her our business and the contract that needed to be drafted for licensing of our products to Flair. Amory's had particular expertise in the area of licensing and intellectual property rights but because of the hurried nature of what we needed, Flair were up against it time-wise if they were to prepare the product for January's fair, Sharon, much to her credit, refused the work because she would not be able to apply herself to it in time for what we wanted. However, Sharon was very interested in what we were doing and asked us to explain our products to her. One thing led to another and by the time we had finished chatting, Sharon had heard not just about the product but also about our lives, as the two were so inextricably entwined. This woman had a heart of gold and without once mentioning money or knowing how our circumstances were going to pan out, she agreed to take care of my family law issues.

Luz and I couldn't believe it; we had gone to Sharon's office to discuss the contract with Flair and had left with first-class representation for my family law matters. Sharon really is one in a million and over the years the kindness and understanding both of her and of her colleague Marion Campbell have been a great comfort to Luz and I. Somehow we had been guided to another good person who could help us in our struggle to succeed.

It was already November 2005 when we had presented our products to Flair and, with the 2006 UK Toy Fair taking place at the end of January, it was all hands to the pumps as we worked with them to have the product prepared for presentation at the fair. It was only because we had developed the prototypes of our products to such a high standard and had the names, logos, trademarks and patents in place that Flair could attempt to work it into the Toy Fair schedule at such short notice. As Paper FX was going to be the brand name, we had to come up with a name for the product itself. What better name than *Dream Weaver*?

We all did our part. Flair worked frantically to have the products Paper FX Dream Weaver and Tumba included in their 2006 catalogue and worked on producing packaging and PR for the products. Luz and I found ourselves buried in magazines and other forms of waste paper as we worked around the clock to produce samples of the output from Paper FX Dream Weaver for the toy fair display stand. We even recruited my mother and my sister Lorraine to help us with the preparation of the paper. Had anyone looked in through the front window of our house, I am sure they would have thought we had some sort of sweatshop in operation!

It was hard to believe, as all four of us sat there tearing and weaving waste paper, that all of this had come about because Luz and I did not have the money to buy a birthday card for my sister. I remembered back to when we had made 150 coasters for Smurfit's and how, after sealing them with PVA glue, we had hung them up to dry on lines of string that stretched from one end of our room to the other, and later went to sleep on the floor of that room with them drying over our heads. I remembered my mother coming into Luz and me with pancakes piled like mountains on a plate to keep us going as we worked through the small hours of the morning on our business plan and our products.

But above everything else, I could not ignore the incredible sequence of extraordinary events that had led us to this point in our lives. Deciding to go to Eason's bookstore on that particular day – if I had not, then I never would have met Luz. Reaching for that book, looking away and losing my concentration, because I thought I heard someone call my name, just at the very moment that Luz reached for it. Then Luz had told me some time later that she had prayed the night before for God to send her a man who would really love her. Then there was the fact that we had invented this product as a result of not having money for a birthday card. Luz knew nothing about inventions, but I did; and I knew nothing about weaving, but Luz did. Without meeting each other, this never could have happened. How watching *The Apprentice* on TV had resulted in us sourcing our product designers. Being in Liffey Valley Shopping Centre and reading the property page of a newspaper, even though we did not have a penny to our name, and then viewing a house that just happened to lead us to Gerry and then to Dónall. The chance way that I found Sharon Scally to take care of my family law matters.

And then there was the weirdest one of all. When we had received our salary, we saved the money to go to the Philippines. Luz had not been home to see her children or her family in more than five years and I was also anxious to meet them. It was a great time with lots of happiness, and for once in Luz's life, her tears in the Philippines were tears of joy. While we were there, we sat on a beach trying to think of a new name for our product called "Topple", something pretty spooky happened. We had been informed that the name Topple was already in use and that we had to come up with an alternative and quickly. We had chosen the name Topple because the game consists of blocks of wood that, if they are built incorrectly, will collapse and fall down. On the beach, I got out my pencil and some paper and started writing down some words as abstract thoughts. The game required balance, so I wrote down the word "Balance"; the blocks would topple or tumble if they fell down, so I wrote the word "Tumble". Next, I took the first three letters of the word "tumble" and wrote them down and then joined the first two letters of the word "balance" to them. It gave me a made-up word spelled T.U.M.B.A. "Tumba, tumba." I kept saying the word over and over in my mind and I liked the sound of it.

Luz then looked over my shoulder and asked me, "How do you know the word 'tumba', honey?"

"I don't know it, sweetheart. It's just a word I have made up to try to replace Topple." I explained to her how the word had been derived for the words "tumble" and "balance".

"You are not going to believe this, honey, and the hairs are standing on the back of my neck, but 'tumba' is a Filipino word – and do you know what it means?" Luz asked, looking at me almost in disbelief. "It means *falling down*," she said in answer to her own question.

I looked back at her in equal disbelief. I had been looking for a word to replace "topple" and on a beach in the Philippines – not anywhere else in the world – I had made up a word from two English words, which turned out to be a Filipino word meaning topple or falling down! What were the odds of that happening? It was and still remains just too weird for words.

Taken in isolation, you could call any one of these incidents a coincidence, but when you put them all together like this and looked at them as part of a bigger picture, then it is not so easy to label them or dismiss them as simply coincidences. Perhaps the thing to do is not to try to understand them, but just to accept them and hope that they continue because up to now they have brought only happiness into our lives.

When we had finished the samples and delivered them to Flair, there was nothing left for us to do except wait for 24 January and the start of the 2006 UK International Toy Fair. Flair had asked us to attend the toy fair and demonstrate both Paper FX and Tumba for the retail buyers attending. As the date drew ever closer, we realised that success or failure, and everything that we had worked for over the past three years, would hang on our demonstration of the products. We would get only one shot at each of the major buyers as they worked their way through the stands of the competing exhibitors, selecting their products for the coming year. Every major retailer in the toy business had their buyers at the fair and they had the power to make or break a product before it even got out of the starting blocks.

But we had one very encouraging piece of news before the fair even started, and it left us smiling. Flair had made an appointment to visit the buyers from Argos and talk to them about some of their new lines. During the course of the meeting, one of the women from Flair placed a bag in which she was carrying some items for the meeting on top of the table. As the meeting was drawing to a close, one of the buyers passed comment on the bag, saying how cool it looked and asking where she had bought it. Laughing, the representative from Flair passed her the bag and asked her to look at it closely. The buyer couldn't believe it – the bag was one that Luz and I had made using the Paper FX Dream Weaver and it was made from a discarded *Argos catalogue*! The buyer could not believe the strength and the professional look of the bag. She commented that it was something you would expect to see for sale in the high street. That was how Argos became our customer.

We arrived at the Excel Exhibition Centre in London's Docklands, the venue for the fair, the day before it was due to start. We had never attended a toy fair before, let alone exhibit at one, and we wanted to familiarise ourselves with the surroundings. Every hotel was booked out to capacity months before the event. For the next four days, Excel would become the playing field for a game where the losers may never again get a throw of the dice and where the rewards for the winners would be anything but child's play.

The day of the fair arrived and the excitement in the air was electric. As we climbed the steps that led into the exhibition centre, I turned to Luz and hugged her. "Well, sweetheart, this is it, everything that we have worked for and every dream we have dreamed will find its truth inside those doors, so let's go in there and fight for our lives."

Perhaps it was because those words were so true – that our lives, our very future, would be decided here today – that I did not feel even the slightest bit nervous as the first of the buyers was escorted to our demonstration area. The buyers would usually have appointments made with the different toy companies and on arrival at a particular toy company's stand, they would be escorted by a member of staff and introduced to the product lines and in particular their new product ranges. Funny as it may seem, we had not rehearsed our pitch to the buyers. All we had with us were some partially finished items, which showed the various stages involved in the making of the objects. Flair had set up a backdrop with the samples we had made for them and a table with the prototype of the Paper FX Dream Weaver displayed on it and for our use.

We had lived with the product for so long that there was nothing about it that we could not explain or convey, even with our eyes closed. Our demonstration technique was to be ourselves and to try to recreate the "wow" factor that I had experienced that day three years earlier when I had first set eyes on the birthday card. And just like that day, we would lead the buyers step-by-step into the world of Paper FX as Luz had done with me, revealing the magic in the process. This was more than demonstrating – we were sharing our love and our passion for what we had created. It was this honesty and passion that seemed to make such a huge impression with the buyers, as one by one they said to us, "Well done, that was a great demonstration and this is a great product." Almost every one of them said to us that the Paper FX Dream Weaver was the most original and innovative new product they had seen in the entire exhibition.

The comments were great, but more importantly they were also being translated into orders as the staff members from Flair kept coming over to us, saying, "This is a huge hit; the orders are rolling in." I don't think we moved from the spot where we stood performing the demonstration that day for more than fifteen minutes, such was the demand to see the Paper FX Dream Weaver as word of our product spread. Luz and I were so high on the success of what was happening, I really think we could have stayed rooted to that spot for the four days of the exhibition without it ever causing us a thought.

When we got back to our hotel room that evening and the door closed behind us, alone for the first time that day, with the exhibition centre, the buyers and the trade left behind, we hugged each other and cried tears of joy, releasing the tension that the uncertainty of the previous three years had built up. We had done it. Despite all the personal tragedy and hardship that had been our lives, despite all of the people who refused to believe in us and our dream, and because of the deep love we shared and the support of the most wonderful family to which we belonged, we had achieved the seemingly impossible. From the front room of my mother's house, penniless, with our belief in each other the only currency of value that we possessed, we had conceived a dream, made it a reality and then brought it to the world stage, making it a success. It had taken a lot of courage and the intervention of some extraordinary, even supernatural events to help it along. But more important than that, we had dared to dream a dream that would change our lives. It can be scary to believe in your dreams when you are penniless, broken and alone, because if they too desert you, what is left?

As we lay on the bed, shoes kicked off and savouring the moment, I began to contemplate the journey we had made. As always when I begin thinking like this, I grabbed some paper and a pencil and started to scribble, trying to capture those thoughts. A picture may paint a thousand words, but sometimes a few words can paint the most beautiful picture.

Dreams are dreamed by dreamers and so I dared to dream
Of moonlit skies, of lovers' sighs and things I've never seen
Dreams are dreamed by dreamers and in my dreams I dream
That this is my reality, that this is not a dream.

When I put the pencil down, I looked at Luz who, exhausted, had fallen asleep on the bed beside me and I thought, *How strange this moment. How strange the merging of the reality and the dream.*

The remaining three days of the fair were a repeat of the first day, with the reaction to the Paper FX Dream Weaver surpassing everyone's expectations. Tumba also received a very good reception.

The UK Toy Fair was just one of many events at which we showcased our products that year. Flair had made a deal with an Australian toy distributor for our products in that territory and together they invited Luz and me as their guests, at their expense, to fly to Australia and repeat our demonstration for them at the Australian Toy Fair. It was being held in the Olympic Stadium in Sydney and we were booked into a lovely hotel in the beautiful Darling Harbour area. Again we received a great response to the product.

When the fair was finished we were brought on a cruise down Sydney Harbour, docking at the Opera House for the duration of our meal and then having drinks above deck as we headed back to the hotel under the starlit sky. We laughed so much as we mingled with the movers and shakers within the business on board the cruise ship, especially when we remembered that back home in Ireland when this dream started we had been sleeping on the floor and then on a desk. And as we drank champagne with the ship passing under the Sydney Harbour Bridge, we spoke about the time we had to count the cents one-by-one to pay for a litre of milk, never imagining at the time that we would one day be recalling it like this.

Australia was another wonderful experience, and it also gave us one more bizarre story to add to our ever-growing catalogue. We had decided to walk a particular route one morning, on our way to take a bus to bring us to the fair. As we did so, we passed by a park. It seemed a nice place to take a picture. As Luz stood beside a signpost for the picture and I got her into the sights of the camera, I suddenly stopped, not believing what I was seeing. The name of the park on the signpost was Tumbalong Park! If someone was sending us signs, they were getting more graphic by the day.

With all of the trade fairs finished for another year, it was time for the marketing people to work on the advertising and promotion for the products in advance of the busiest time of the year, which was of course Christmas. In August of 2006 we received an e-mail from our distributor Flair. Tumba had just won the UK Science Museum's Award for "Smart Play" in their smart toy awards. Luz and I were delighted. The system of awarding the points to the competing products was based on fifty per cent of the scoring coming from eminent scientists and people involved in science, and the other fifty per cent coming from children who participated in a sleepover event in the museum and played with the toys. I have loved science all of my life, so to receive an award from the Science Museum was something special for me. But what made it even more rewarding was the fact that the inventing of Tumba involved the working out of and application of a mathematical formula. I had only achieved basic secondary school education, finishing in my third year after completing my Group Certificate. It went a long way to prove that, when you want to do something, you can do it.

Tumba is an extraordinary product. It consists of a set of sixty rectangular blocks, each block divided into six equal sections. Each section is coloured one of five colours: red, yellow, green, blue or orange. All of the blocks contain the same colours, but none of the blocks have the colours applied in the same sequence. The game is simple: you try to build all sixty blocks following one simple rule – "colour on colour". It literally takes a minute to learn how to play Tumba, but many lifetimes will not be enough to master it. Gary McGuire, Professor of Mathematics at University College Dublin, was enthralled with Tumba, and wrote a paper on the game which threw up some extraordinary facts. Remember, the object of the game is to build all sixty blocks without them falling down. To quote Professor McGuire's paper, there are 10^{42} ways to complete Tumba. To put this in context, there are 10^{19} permutations of the Rubik's cube, which is tiny in comparison, and 10^{26} metres from one end of the universe to the other! Empirical estimates show that the number of ways to complete Tumba is much higher, and could be equal to the number of particles in the universe. If everyone on earth played Tumba a billion times each, the odds are overwhelmingly small that any two of those completions would be the same. If Tumba were to be built in zero-gravity conditions, the number of completed builds would be 8.9×10^{90}. This is more than a billion times greater than the number of particles in the known universe, which is estimated to be 10^{80}. Taking into account different ways of playing each block, it is possible that the number of completions could be 10^{100}, a number known as a googol. Now, here is the beauty of Tumba: to complete even one of these builds is a challenge and when a player does complete a build, they will most certainly be looking at a structure that no one has ever seen before or will ever see again when it is collapsed.

We were just coming down to earth after the Science Museum award when in October we were notified that the Toy Retailers Association in the UK had chosen the Paper FX Dream Weaver as one of their Dream Toys for Christmas 2006, which meant it was one of the most sought-after toys that year. The Paper FX Dream Weaver was one of what is called the "cool dozen" toys, with some of the others including such names as Trivial Pursuit, Barbie, Bratz, Dr Who and Thomas the Tank Engine. These were all properties of multi-million pound companies like Hasbro, Mattel and Vivid – and now sitting alongside them was our Paper FX Dream Weaver. Who would have believed it?

The publicity created when the product was selected as a Dream Toy was phenomenal. We appeared in newspapers in the UK and Ireland and took part in radio interviews, the most notable being John Murray's *The Business* show on RTÉ. John cleared the decks and devoted the entire show to us. Following from John's show, the Paper FX Dream Weaver appeared on the *Late Late Toy Show* where it got such a great reaction that the following week we appeared on the show ourselves for an interview with its host, Pat Kenny.

It was an incredible time in our life. Following our interviews on the radio and TV, complete strangers were coming up to us on the street anywhere we went, shaking our hands or slapping us on the back, congratulating us and telling us how much they admired us and how we had inspired so many of them not to give up on their dreams. It was truly humbling. E-mails of congratulation came in not just from Ireland but from all over the world. Then there were all of the e-mails from people from all walks of life, housewives, solicitors, professors – everyone and anyone looking for help and guidance with their idea or invention.

The most rewarding of these was an invitation from Diarmuid Timmons from the Institute of Technology, Sligo, who asked us to give a talk to his design students and also to the final-year business students. It was a pleasure dealing with Diarmuid, whose love of design and dedication to his students was very clear to see. The students were delightful and it tickled them a lot to know we were lecturing them without any formal qualifications to our name. We hope it proved to them what application and dedication can achieve. I was so proud of Luz that day. She was a Filipina in a foreign country, English not her first language, and yet the students after hearing her speak gave her a standing ovation. Her children would have been so proud of their mother.

It was such a buzz to go walking around the stores of the country and to see our products with our names on the back stocked and taking pride of place on the shelves. Toymaster, Smyth's, Argos, Nimble Fingers and World of Wonder were just some of the outlets stocking the products in Ireland. When we flew to London, we pinched ourselves in disbelief as we walked around Harrods, John Lewis and Hamleys, to name but a few of the stores stocking our products. It was also available through Argos, Tesco, Boots and numerous online shops. Then there was the excitement of turning on the TV and flicking through the channels and seeing the advertisements for Paper FX Dream Weaver.

Christmas 2006 came and the product sold out, with waiting lists for it in some stores. It was a very satisfying end to an unbelievable year and it was no sooner over than we prepared ourselves once again for the 2007 UK Toy Fair. The fair was held in the same venue, but this time Luz and I did not have to spend as much time demonstrating; the buyers knew the product now, so we spent our time mixing and networking, getting to know various people within the industry.

Every year the Toy Retailers Association hold their "Toy of the Year" awards, a very prestigious, well-attended event. To win an award is a highly prized accolade within the business; you could almost say that they are like the Oscars of the toy industry. Luz and I did not attend the event. Our product had only been available from August 2006, so we did not have a full year to make an impact. Most products would have been available from January but, because we had not been to Flair until November of the previous year, there had been a lot of work to do before the product was ready to manufacture. Instead, we had a night out with Steve Lennon, swapped notes on the fair and caught up on some news on other projects we were contemplating.

The following morning it was breakfast as usual and then over to Flair's stand at the fair. However, this time when we arrived, we noticed an unusual amount of activity for that hour of the morning. When we came to the notice of the staff from Flair, they said, "Hi, Noel and Luz, can you come this way? Peter needs to talk with you." Peter Brown is the CEO of Flair Leisure Products plc. Luz and I did not know what was happening, it was all so unusual. Peter Brown met us in his usual understated manner. Smiling, he presented us with a framed certificate and said, "Congratulations, Noel and Luz! The Paper FX Dream Weaver won the Creative Toy of the Year award at last night's event."

We were speechless. Our product, which had only been available for five months of that year, had beaten all the competition and come away with the award. We were delighted, not just for ourselves, but for Dónall, Gerry and of course for Flair. As we left London for Dublin, I think we may have been able to fly home without the assistance of the plane, so high were we on the success of our win.

When we got home, there were more radio and newspaper interviews. We were also now in discussions through Flair with a major European manufacturer and distributor of toys, puzzles and games called Ravensburger, who were looking for the rights to distribute our product in at least twenty-nine territories. We eventually did the deal through Flair with Ravensburger and they set to work on producing a new version of the Paper FX Dream Weaver called Paper Creation for the European market.

More awards followed. The Paper FX Dream Weaver was awarded best new UK Hobby Design by the British Toy and Hobby Association in their annual Max-It Awards for Excellence in Design. This was the third award for the

Paper FX Dream Weaver, but a fourth was on the way. The *Good Toy Guide* awarded it a Gold Medal in their annual toy awards. Then Tumba came back into the picture when it was shortlisted, alongside the Nintendo Wii, for the Best Non-UK Game Design in the Max-It awards, with no winner being announced as the judges could not agree on their decision. It was an incredible run of accolades for our products:

The Dream Toy Award
Creative Toy of the Year Award
Max-It Award
Good Toy Guide Gold Medal
Science Museum Smart Play Award
Max-It shortlist for Tumba, no winner announced.

25

Weaving Dreams

Luz

Summer of 2007 was really special for us. Two of my children, Charmie, the eldest in the family, and Herlene, the second youngest, were finally able to come to Ireland and visit us. They were accompanied by Adelyn, my niece, and Pamela, my very good friend. They stayed with us for three months and it was a great time for us all to get to know each other better.

Because Charmie had been conceived in violence when I was just a teenager, I had experienced no feelings of love towards her when she was a baby. In fact, it would be true to say that I hated her. I hated my own daughter, my own child. She was the living proof of my torment and pain and a constant reminder of the animal who had abused me. As the frustrations of the abuse and violence in that marriage overpowered me, I in turn vented those frustrations on Charmie by hitting her. Every time I recalled how I had abused Charmie, I would be consumed by the guilt and shame of what I had done. I would cry my heart out with regret, but the tears, no matter how genuine, could not undo the hurt I had caused.

Noel tried to comfort me by explaining that I had also been abused and that I was really only a child having a child when I gave birth to Charmie. He would tell me that it was not my fault, that my head had been messed up and that I should be so proud that I remained sane after surviving that horrible time in my life. Noel said that no one would condemn me for what I had done and everyone would understand how that could happen. He asked me if I had ever sat down with Charmie and really discussed this matter with her. I hadn't and I didn't know how. Charmie was in her twenties now, married and a mother; she would understand, Noel told me, but only if I explained everything to her.

As a mother it was heart-warming to feel the respect that my children had for me, particularly when you consider how little time I had to spend with them growing up. It was so lovely for Charmie, Herlene and me to be spending time together like this, but nice as all this was, I knew that there was still some invisible barrier stopping Charmie and me from really letting go and fully expressing our love for each other.

One day while I was upstairs with Adelyn, Herlene and Pamela, Noel came up and told me that Charmie, who was on her own in the kitchen and doing some baking, wanted to see me for a moment. I didn't know it at the time, but Noel had taken the initiative while Charmie was on her own to tell her of my deep regret for how I had treated her and of how much I really loved her.

When I walked into the kitchen, Noel surprised me by saying, "You two have some talking to do." Then he left, closing the door behind him.

Charmie spoke first. "Ma, I really love you and I understand why you treated me the way that you did. Daddy Noel has explained it all to me and I am so sorry for everything that you have suffered." The tears were welling up in her eyes as she spoke. "I just missed you, Ma, I missed being hugged and I missed not having your love. I never knew the love of a father and with you gone I never really had a mother. I was not Hermie's daughter and he never made me feel welcome in your house. It was so hard when you were gone, Ma, I was really alone."

"Oh, Charmie, I am so sorry for everything you have suffered. If I could go back and make it different I would, but I am here now and you will never be without me in your life again."

We hugged and we cried and we let out all of the pent-up emotions that we had never been able to release.

Charmie was a married woman now, a mother with a child of her own, but as I held her close and stroked her hair, her tears trickling down my neck, she was simply Charmie my daughter. For the first time since she was born, I thought of her and held her in my arms, not as just my daughter but as my little girl.

Charmie, Richard and I – the three of us were finally coming to terms with and healing wounds that had remained open for far too long. We were healing ourselves and in that process healing each other. So many times I have thanked Noel for making all of this happen, but he will not hear of it and replies, "I only supplied the bandages, Luz; you guys healed yourselves." No wonder my kids love that man so much.

Charmie told me, "You know, Ma, Daddy Noel really is the father I always dreamed of having as a little girl and now he is here in our lives and I love him so much." And again we both burst into tears as we realised the goodness that was now in our life.

Noel

When I opened the door and peeped into the sitting-room, the most wonderful sight greeted me. Luz and Charmie were sitting on the couch hugging each other, both of them crying tears of happiness and release as the hurt of over twenty years was washed away. Both of them had been victims of a brutal man, but they were victims no longer. Now they were survivors, mother and daughter, and the deep love they had for each other was beautiful to see.

Later that evening, Charmie came to talk to me. Giving me a hug, she said, "Thank you, Dad, for loving my Mama the way that you do, and thank you for coming into our lives. You are the father I always dreamed about but never knew. I love you, Dad, and I'm so proud to be your daughter." A few more tears were added to the copious flow already seen that day.

I have gained a wonderful family in Luz's children and I am so proud and touched by the respect every one of them shows to me. Sometimes when I see Luz with them or hear her talking with them over the phone, I get a little sad and wish that I could see and talk to my kids like that, share in their lives and be a father to them. But the choice is not mine, so I have learned to accept what I cannot change. I love my children dearly and despite what misguided views they might have about me, I will always love them. Nothing they or anyone can say or do will stop me from loving them. I may never see them again and if that is their wish, then I have to accept that. My heart has already been broken by their absence in my life, so there is nothing more of it to break. My son is a twenty-two-year-old man now and my daughter is a nineteen-year-old woman. I cannot tell them what to do or make them love me if they don't, but whatever happens I have the memory locked away in my heart of my little boy and my little girl sitting on my knee, their arms wrapped around my neck, hugging me so tightly and telling me, "We love you, Daddy." That is what I hold onto and nothing or no one can ever take that away from me.

As 2008 goes on, we are looking forward to new versions of our products being released throughout Ireland, the UK and the rest of Europe. This year we also hope to see distribution in America. We are also working on some very exciting new products and are already in talks with companies with regard to their commercialisation. But as rewarding as all of this commercial success has been, there is one thing which, if we can achieve it, will give a far greater meaning to our own personal happiness and what has happened in our lives.

When I arrived in the Philippines with Luz, it was the first time I had ever travelled to South East Asia and, to be honest, I did not know what to expect when I got there. I have always loved adventure and for me this trip *was* an adventure to a part of the world that seemed exotic and mysterious. It was obvious from the moment I set foot in the Philippines that there was a huge amount of poverty in the country. During the ride from Davao airport to Luz's sister's house and later to our hotel, it was clear to see how the struggle for life was a losing battle for the poor who lived there. The hospitality I received from the people of Davao to this day has remained unmatched by any country I have ever visited. No matter where I went, I was welcomed and offered a share in whatever was available to eat, even though for so many people it was an obvious struggle to put that food on the table. The people were generous, accommodating and extraordinarily resourceful, but the children just stole my heart away.

We had been staying in a five-star hotel in Davao, which was costing us the equivalent of a budget holiday in Spain. It was of course a nice novelty at first, being surrounded by all of this luxury and treated like a king and queen, but there was something of a siege mentality about the place. It seemed to be occupied for the most part by wealthy foreigners who, for one reason or another, had business in Davao but who confined themselves to the hotel as a barrier and a sign of their disdain for the world outside. It was too elitist for Luz's and my blood and we were finding it increasingly difficult to reconcile living in this luxury when a few hundred yards away, we could encounter street kids who looked like they were famished.

With Luz as my guide, we were able to leave the recommended safe tourist areas and venture into the real

Davao with the real people. It was while out on these excursions that we encountered the wretched poor of the city and our hearts would break when we saw them and how they struggled to feed themselves and their children. Education was not an option. Then there were the children who seemed to have no one to care for them, their emaciated bodies defying the laws of nature as they somehow managed to stand upright, fighting their way to the front of the others like them in their efforts to beg a few pesos from us. For the first time in my life, I had encountered real poverty and it disturbed me greatly.

When we got back to the hotel, Luz and I overhauled the budget we had set aside for our holiday and quickly realised that if we moved out of the luxury hotel into a more modest and cheaper hotel, away from the usual tourist spots, then we could make considerable savings. So we checked out and made the move.

It was lovely to see Luz here in Davao among her own people. She had so much history here and it was good to finally be able to identify with the people and places she had spoken of when we first met. I loved it there. Yes, for sure there was an edge to the place; police were armed and every time you entered a public building or shopping mall you were frisked for guns or other weapons, but after a while you got used to that. To be honest, I felt a lot safer there in Davao than I would walking some Dublin streets at night. Although Davao is a city where you need to keep your wits about you, it had been transformed from the lawlessness and anarchy that Luz had previously experienced into one of the most habitable cities in South East Asia. When you asked the locals how this almost miraculous transformation had come about, they would all mention one name: Mayor Rodrigo Duterte. Many questioned his often controversial methods, which saw him being accused of heading death squads that would more or less mete out an uncompromising and final punishment for those who broke the law. Whatever the truth or not of the accusations levelled against him, few could dispute the result of his tenure as mayor.

The money we had saved by moving hotels was used by us to help the street kids. The joy we experienced in that simple act of caring, and to experience what it had meant to those children for someone to care, revealed to us what we were meant to do with the rest of our lives and why Luz and I had been brought together. Everything that had happened in our lives from the moment that Luz and I met had led us to this moment and this revelation. Nothing that we had achieved – the awards, the little bit of fame or the feeling of having money in our pocket – could compare to the feelings of absolute joy we experienced when we saw the smiles on the faces of those children and the knowledge that we had it within us to change their lives.

As we got to know the children and spoke to them and their families, it became apparent that the one thing they all wanted was an education. They realised that education was a key that could open the door to another world, a world in which they would have a chance and the *hope* of a better life. It has inspired Luz and I to register our own charity, called the Noel and Luz Foundation, and our ambition in time is to build schools where these children and children like them will have access to free education and will be provided with a decent meal at least once a day.

We spoke with a representative of the mayor's office and discussed our plans with them and we hope that in the very near future we can work with them to help in the delivering of education to underprivileged children in Davao. We have also been talking to Mayor Lumayag, the Mayor of Polomolok, South Cotabato, about providing these schools, and his response was fantastic. He immediately set aside three and a half hectares of land for our use for the project.

We hope that the continued success of the Paper FX Dream Weaver, Paper Creation and Tumba, as well as other products we hope to introduce to the market, will secure our lives financially and allow Luz and me to dedicate our lives to caring for these children.

We all need money to survive in this world – such is the nature of our society – but Luz and I will never be motivated purely by the accumulation of money. Yes, for sure we know the stresses and the strains of not having money, but to be motivated purely by its accumulation is to us an empty pursuit. We are motivated by success, not just in the business sense, but in the success we have made of our relationship and the deep love and respect we have for each other.

I can recall living in a 3,500-square-foot house situated on an acre of land, with double garages the size of some people's homes, and still being the most miserable man in the world. And yet when I was sleeping on a hard floor in the corner of a room in my mother's house, the cold draughts biting at my skin and not a penny to my name, I was the happiest man in the world. I was happy because whatever I had *now* was real. It was not an illusion of grandeur owned by the banks, building societies or other borrowed money. It was me, brought back down to my most exposed self, and it forced me to look at myself in ways I never would have done before.

But the most real thing in my life is Luz. Her love, compassion and understanding are the real currency of my life. Luz has brought to me happiness that is as immeasurable as the love I have for her. Unselfish to a fault, her capacity for giving has no bounds and what she has given of herself to me sustained me through the most difficult time in my life and nourished my soul until I was whole again. And I am whole again because Luz is now an inseparable part of me and I an inseparable part of her. There is no Noel without Luz and there is no Luz without Noel. Whatever we have now in our lives we have built together and from nothing we changed the course of our lives.

We have a long way to go before we see the fruits of our labours but we have at last set in motion something which we hope will secure our future and in so doing secure the lives of disadvantaged children. We are living proof that nothing in this world is impossible to achieve if you want it badly enough and are motivated by the right reasons. Whatever happens with the business from here on in is down to our dedication and hard work and to a large extent it is in the hands of God. But God has been good to Noel and Luz since we met and we have every reason to believe that He will continue to smile down upon us.

The multi-award-winning Paper FX Dream Weaver and Paper Creation are now sold throughout Europe, the UK and Ireland, with America our next port of call. The award-winning and amazing Tumba is sold in Ireland, the UK, America and Japan.

We have come a long way on this journey. Just how far was demonstrated when we stood in Davao airport on our way back home after our visit to the Philippines to see Luz's children, our children. Standing in front of a semi-transparent pane of glass that formed part of the terminal wall, Luz asked me, "What can you see in the glass, Noel?"

I looked at the glass and, seeing our reflection, I said, "I can see you and me, sweetheart. Why do you ask?"

Hugging me ever so tight and turning her head to once again look at the glass, Luz replied, "I see the little sixteen-year-old girl in the white majorette's uniform standing beside her prince and she is smiling back so happily at me."

The Paper FX Dream Weaver has woven more dreams than we ever could have imagined.

About the Authors

Noel Donegan was born in Dublin, Ireland, in 1960. He has lived in Ireland all his life and is the father of two children. He is the inventor of Easi-Perm, a hairdressing invention which was licensed to L'Oréal, and is also the joint inventor of the multi-award-winning arts and crafts phenomena, the Paper FX Dream Weaver and Paper Creation. He is the joint inventor of the award-winning game/puzzle Tumba. He now shares his life and weaves his dreams with the love of his life, Luz Java.

Luz Java was born in Lambajon, Baganga, Davao Oriental, Philippines, in 1964. She is the mother of five children and the proud grandmother of two grandchildren. She is the joint inventor of the multi-award-winning arts and crafts phenomena the Paper FX Dream Weaver and Paper Creation. She is the joint inventor of the award-winning game/puzzle Tumba. After a varied career, which included travelling the world working onboard the Cunard Line cruise ships, she settled in Dublin in 2001. She now shares her dreams and weaves her life with the love of her life, Noel Donegan.

Acknowledgements

Among the many people that we are indebted to in the preparation of this book and their contribution to our life story, we wish to express particular thanks to Margaret Donegan and Lorraine Harper. Their love, kindness and generosity sustained us through all the difficult times and made everything that we now do possible. We are especially indebted to Gerry Kinsella and Dónall Curtin, who believed in us and supported us when no one else would. Steve Lennon's advice and guidance was of such great help to us, but more importantly, we thank him for being a good friend and standing by us.

Solicitors Susan Battye, Michael Walshe and Sharon Scally deserve not just our thanks but medals of honour for their kindness and understanding, which was so much above the call of duty. Gearoid Schutte, our patent agent and all-round great guy gave us terrific advice and so understood our impoverished circumstances when dealing with us. Thanks to Gay Mitchell MEP, his wife Norma and all his staff for the Trojan efforts they made on our behalf. James Kelly, our landlord and a great guy, gave us so much space and time when things were tough; thanks so much, James. We owe a special debt of gratitude to John

Murray and Pat Kenny for introducing our products and us to the people of Ireland and for being just fantastic guys who took a genuine interest in our lives. We're grateful to Brian Langan and the great people at Poolbeg Press for their patience and guidance, taking us by the hand and helping us to realise another one of our dreams.

But the biggest debt of gratitude that we owe belongs to the book we never read and which sat on the shelves of Eason's bookstore in O'Connell Street. Without that book or that store, none of this would be happening.